W9-DFO-585

WHAT PEOPLE ARE SAYING
ABOUT *INSIDE OUT*

"I can't think of better people to write a book on servant leadership than the Wilkersons. In my years in the White House, I saw Rich lead with grace and kindness, and I believe this book will help bring out the extraordinary leader in all of us. It's a conversation that is sorely needed in Washington politics, and across the country as well."

—JOSHUA DUBOIS
Former White House Head of the President's Faith Based
Initiative under President Barack Obama

"I loved this book, and I love the authors Rich and Robyn Wilkerson. They don't just write about servant leadership, they live and breathe it every day. Their passion for serving others and developing servant leaders is inspiring and I'm thankful they have chosen to share this book and their wisdom with the world."

—JON GORDON
Bestselling author of *The Energy Bus* and *The Seed*

"There is no greater calling than serving your community. And when coupled with the ability to lead through selflessness and compassion, it becomes a transformational force. Rich and Robyn Wilkerson have demonstrated these traits and have shown that people rooted in values and committed to God can change lives."

—SIMON CRUZ
President & CEO, Intercredit Bank, Miami, Florida

"The Wilkersons of Miami are the embodiment of servant leadership. They have the drive and the personal characteristics of faithfulness, integrity, and selflessness—to name just a few—that are required of all servant leaders. By way of servant leadership they have led Trinity to be one of the largest predominantly Haitian churches in the world."

—DENNIS HAMMOND
President and CEO of SANDPOINTE, LLC, West Palm Beach, Florida

"I consider Rich and Robyn Wilkerson as my second parents. They are the epitome of servant leadership. Their loyalty, compassion, and mentoring in my life have forever changed me. Saying I was eager to read a book like this would be an understatement."

—JASON KENNEDY
ENews host, Hollywood, California

"The Wilkersons have profoundly impacted my life. Rich is one of the most gifted communicators and leaders I've ever met. He leads with humble boldness. He communicates with holy humor. Rich is a one-of-a-kind voice to our generation that must be heard."

—MARK BATTERSON
Bestselling author of *Primal* and *The Circle Maker;* lead pastor, National Community Church, Washington, DC

"Rich and Robyn Wilkerson have modeled servant leadership for as long as I have known them. Their years of leading social justice in Miami through Trinity Church and Peacemakers is well documented. They impacted us here at Planetshakers in a profound way. Rich was instrumental in seeing our conference grow from 300 to 20,000 through the years. This book will challenge, inspire, and empower you to reach your dreams."

—RUSSELL EVANS
Founder and CEO of Panetshakers, Melbourne, Australia

"How God and others perceive us in His kingdom is directly correlated to our hearts' desire to serve others. Having known Rich and Robyn Wilkerson for many decades, they have modeled what I believe to be the key ingredient in servant leadership—sacrifice."

—DR. RICHARD D. NELSON
Founder and chairman of the board of Plant Sciences, Inc.,
Watsonville, California

"Rich and Robyn Wilkerson have been friends for over twenty years, and I have known them to be people who are transparent, authentic, and who love people across all cultures. This book is about how that can happen where you are."

—CHRISTINE CAINE
Founder A21 Campaign, Sydney, Australia

"Servant leadership is what is desperately needed in our world and once embraced should never be departed from. In this book, *Inside Out,* my friends Rich and Robyn Wilkerson present a great read that will help keep servant leadership authentically grounded and real."

—GARY CLARKE
Lead pastor, Hillsong, London, UK

"The Wilkersons embody the idea of twenty-first century God-centered servant leadership. This book, *Inside Out,* empowers the reader with kingdom principles of servant leadership that facilitate a platform by which everyday people truly can become extraordinary leaders."

—SAMMY RODRIGUEZ
President, National Hispanic Christian Leadership Conference

"The rallying mandate for our future demands we adopt the servant leadership tools so perfectly taught in *Inside Out.* The Wilkerson family has had a profound impact on my life, and Rich helped me to cultivate these principles in my personal and professional life over fifteen years ago. This is real! #Robynwasright"

—KEVIN COMPTON
Partner emeritus and co-owner, Kleiner Perkins Caufield &
Byers; Sharks Sports & Entertainment; NHL San Jose Sharks

"This is a beautifully compelling book, full of wisdom to accompany all of us throughout life. The most powerful and important stories in the world are those of people such as Auntie Rie and Pastor O and Mackie and Uncle Tal and Elon and Graham and Allen—and many more. This book is a blessing!"

—DAVID LAWRENCE JR.
Retired publisher of *The Miami Herald* and nationally known
early childhood advocate

"Rich and Robyn are leaders par excellence, so we need to learn everything that God has laid on their hearts about discovering our roles as servant leaders in *Inside Out.* As a cognitive neuroscientist, I always teach that there is something you can do that no one else can . . . so that makes you a leader! This great book will help you recognize and apply this truth."

—DR. CAROLINE LEAF
Cognitive neuroscientist, speaker, author of *Who Switched off my Brain,* host of the TV show *Switch on Your Brain*

"'Brother Tom, what can I do for you?' It's always the first thing Rich says to me. And the best part of all, it's always heartfelt. Rich and Robyn's new book, *Inside Out,* is a powerful testimony of Ephesians 6, "Whatever good anyone does, he will receive the same from the Lord." Just meeting Rich and Robyn has expanded my vision to live a greater, fuller life—a life that comes from living generously. Our world is better for this message! I know this firsthand."

—TOM NEWMAN
Founder/president of Impact Productions; producer of *End of the Spear, Christmas Child, Home Run,* and *The Christmas Candle*

INSIDE OUT

HOW EVERYDAY PEOPLE
BECOME EXTRAORDINARY LEADERS

———

RICH WILKERSON
ROBYN WILKERSON

Copyright © 2015 by Rich Wilkerson and Robyn Wilkerson
All rights reserved.

Published by Salubris Resources

1445 N. Boonville Ave.

Springfield, Missouri 65802

No portion of this book may be reproduced, stored in a retrieval system, or transmitted in any form or by any means—electronic, mechanical, photocopy, recording, or any other—except for brief quotations in printed reviews, without the prior written permission of the publisher.

Cover design by PlainJoe Studios (www.plainjoestudios.com)
Interior formatting by Prodigy Pixel (www.prodigypixel.com)

Unless otherwise specified, Scripture quotations used in this book are taken from *The Message.* Copyright © 1993, 1994, 1995, 1996, 2000, 2001, 2002. Used by permission of NavPress Publishing Group.

Scriptures marked KJV are from the King James Version, held in public domain.

ISBN: 978-1-68067-036-3

18 17 16 15 • 1 2 3 4

Printed in the United States of America

DEDICATION

———

To the more than 900 registered servant leaders
who help make Trinity Church of Miami
(@trinitymiami) happen every week.
Without your inspiration, this book
would never have been written.
We love you!

—Rich and Robyn

CONTENTS

—

FOREWORD

――――――

IF THERE IS ONE TOPIC that holds a special place in my heart, it is leadership. I've written on the subject, given talks about it, and made every effort to demonstrate the principles of effective leadership in my own life.

Yet, there is a higher level of leadership to which I aspire, and that is servant leadership.

The reason this is so important to me is because I truly believe that today the world is in desperate need of a different leadership role model. We have all seen the negative effects of self-serving leaders—whether they are running countries, businesses, churches, educational institutions, or whatever. We need leaders who are here to serve, not to be served.

Rich and Robyn Wilkerson, the authors of this fast-moving book filled with engaging stories, are no strangers to the power that servanthood can unleash in the lives of those served as well as the lives of the leaders who serve. They've witnessed it in their day-to-day work with families, high school students, and the disenfranchised people they reach out to in the core of Miami, Florida. They've followed servant leaders into hospitals, prisons and high-crime areas, and have served alongside them—with amazing results.

Through the pages of this book, you may discover concrete reasons to both lead and serve, and you may even be inspired by some of the examples to accomplish mighty things you never imagined you could. This book is not about culture, politics, or religion. It's about setting aside differences, forming new bonds with others who choose to meet needs, and taking action when it would probably be more comfortable to "sit it out."

My hope is that, as you read this book, it will become apparent to you that servant leadership is a way of life that's worth pursuing!

—KEN BLANCHARD

Co-author of *The One-Minute Manager*

PREFACE

AFTER MORE THAN FORTY YEARS of marriage, I've learned to trust a woman's intuition. Being married to someone as brilliant as Robyn Marie Buntain Wilkerson has been a learning experience for me. I've learned that she's right when she feels strongly about something. Let me explain.

It was April of 1998. We had been invited to visit Trinity Church in Miami—to discuss the possibility of moving our family from Tacoma, Washington, where we had lived for nearly eighteen years, to South Florida. I wanted Robyn to see the place—and meet the organization that was asking us to come. To be honest with you, I knew she wouldn't like it, and I was asking her to do the worst thing imaginable for a wife and mother. I was asking her to leave all of the security she deserved after four children and twenty-five years of marriage. I was asking her to leave her parents, who lived right next door to us, and I was asking her to leave the place where she was raised. Taking her away from her parents was much worse than pulling a cat off a couch.

Really, nothing could have been more far-fetched than what I was asking of her. Our oldest son, Jonfulton, was entering his senior year in high school. Our second son, Rich, Jr., had more friends than Starbucks has franchises. Our third son, Graham, who had Spinal Meningitis as a baby, was battling brain damage, and our baby, Taylor, was only eight years old.

So on our way to a four-day, get-acquainted time, I promised Robyn that we definitely wouldn't accept an offer while we were there meeting with the board of directors. My goal in making this promise was to give Robyn some peace and comfort that we "probably" wouldn't be moving to Miami. It was also a hedge against us having to reject any offer publicly, so as not to embarrass anyone on either side.

Robyn likes to say that, at that time, we were the perfect "Abercrombie family." We lived in "Whitesville USA"; very sterile, very protected, and very naive. Yet at that same time, I had a tremendous desire for significance. I was forty-five years old and had a successful life in my small circles—but I felt as if, in my life, I had risked absolutely nothing to help people in real need.

I wanted Miami, but at the same time, I must say I was deathly afraid of Miami.

Miami was big. It was cosmopolitan. It wasn't the America that many Americans envision when they think America. Yet, they had me at "Hello!"

The team we would be working with was almost entirely of African descent—some Spanish, but mainly African: African American, Haitian, and Caribbean.

Our mission would be to develop a prototype for helping the disenfranchised of the city that could be replicated across the country. At least that was my original goal. But I was so naive I had little idea what I was even thinking.

Robyn, of course, was not impressed. When she saw the facility in which we would be working, she almost fell over.

She definitely was not impressed with the board of directors—and I guarantee you that the board was not impressed with us, either. Out of nine directors, only one was Anglo (the Miami term for white people). And he was the one director who voted against us! (We still find that mildly amusing.)

The place was a mess. As Robyn likes to say, the termites had locked arms at the elbow to keep the tables and chairs from falling to the ground. But as crummy as it was, it had me.

I must admit that before going on that "get acquainted trip" I had resigned myself that we wouldn't be moving to Miami. At our age, it would be asking way too much of our children—and, in particular, my wife.

But there we were, meeting with the directors. I remember getting back to the two-star hotel in which we were staying and Robyn saying to me, "What are you thinking? Are you out of your mind?"

I replied, "Well at least you're here with me, and even though the hotel isn't that great, it's Miami. Let's look at it as a mini vacation." She wasn't buying it.

We met some wonderful people that week and on Tuesday night, when we hit the sack, I said to Robyn, "Well, it's almost over. One more day and we'll be heading back to our home in the Northwest."

I remember her saying something like, "I can't wait!"

With that being said, there's no way in a million years that I could have prepared for Wednesday morning. At 7:00 a.m., Robyn sat straight up in bed and said, "Rich, I had a dream—or an impression, or something strange in the night—and I believe Miami is our future!"

I tried to shake myself awake, believing that I was still dreaming. Finally, I exclaimed, "Whaaat?"

She said, "Yes, in the coming years, the whole nation is going to look at the large urban centers of America as the future. This country is no longer going to embrace the suburbs. America's cities are going to revive and become massive cultural centers. Miami will be one of the nation's leaders. In fact, we need to move towards diversity and color. Last night, I envisioned us eventually having an African-American president."

I said, "Baby, are you still sleeping? This can't be you."

She responded, "Rich you know me!"

And in that moment, I thought of that "women's intuition thing." She had never been wrong in twenty-five years of marriage. I began to think she might be onto something!

The years since then have been both *hard* and overwhelmingly *fulfilling*. Robyn has joined me in co-authoring this book because she exemplifies the very heart of servant leadership.

The true servant leader is always looking for the bigger picture in every opportunity. It's rarely about *me*—my feelings, my desires, what I want. Rather, it's about how I can help others reach their dreams.

Robyn and I have always operated on a verse from *The Message,* Ephesians 6:7, which essentially says, "What you make happen for others God will make happen for you."

That's servant leadership—making things happen for others through acts of service and kindness.

Anyway, that's how we started here in Miami, in 1998. The board of directors was even more shocked than we were when we told them our intention that day. In fact, it took them two weeks to offer us a formal invitation—which, of course, we accepted.

This all happened because a woman had a dream. And her dream helped my dream become a beautiful reality! Now, after fifteen years and thousands of lives touched, we are experiencing the joy of servant leadership as it manifests itself in our world.

—RICH WILKERSON

INTRODUCTION

—

THERE ARE PEOPLE ALL OVER the world who don't realize they have the potential to become great leaders. They simply live ordinary lives, never grasping for the next rung on the ladder. They stay mostly to themselves in their own private worlds, many of them living their lives unaware of the abilities that are latent within them.

There are other people who don't know much about leadership, but they know how to serve, serve, and serve some more. They are selfless in every way. Their impact is often limited, however, because they haven't worked to develop their inherent leadership skills.

And there are leaders worldwide—in every group, business, organization, or branch of government—who are powerful leaders but who simply don't understand that the way to have the greatest impact as a leader is to become a servant.

The people we've just described may live in your city . . . in your neighborhood . . . next door to you . . . or, in your house. Yes, you guessed it! Those people—any of them—may even be you!

This book is about the why and how of servant leadership. Why it's vitally important, and how to meld leadership and servanthood into something powerful and significant.

Throughout this book, we'll explore the lives of "givers" and "takers," of "successes" and "failures," of people who could have been and done much more with their lives, had they known the principles of *Inside Out*.

We'll also look at very special people you would never have heard of but for a single amazing act of service—or the endless acts of service—they performed. Remarkable people often come from humble backgrounds and become known simply because of the things they willingly and eagerly do for others.

Think about the familiar story of Mother Teresa. She wasn't an upper-level executive of a giant corporation or an elected official in high office. She wasn't a wealthy media star or an eloquent public speaker. She didn't lend her name to a perfume fragrance or a line of designer clothing. In fact, her clothing could be described as the exact opposite of "designer."

No, Mother Teresa was a servant, and a humble one at that. True, she gained global fame, but it wasn't of her choosing. She was simply a small, frail woman who was guided by overwhelming love for the unlovely. She toiled for more than forty-five years among the poorest of the poor, in what is likely the most impoverished city in the world.[1] She lived, and gave, and died in Calcutta, India, surrounded by the people who owed her their very lives.

There probably aren't many among us who are future candidates for the Nobel Peace Prize. We likely won't be the subjects of a report on CNN. There may never be books written about our lives, or movies-of-the-week produced for the Lifetime Network.

Of course, we could be wrong. You could be the next Mother Teresa. The next Nelson Mandela. But it's more likely that you will serve in silence, with little praise or recognition. In fact, it could be that we ourselves are the only ones who know what selfless acts we have performed out of our hearts for service. But that, friends, is enough. It's exactly enough.

Servant leaders serve because it is the right thing to do. Because, as the saying goes, "It is more blessed to give than to receive" (Acts 20:35).

If you are a parent or a grandparent, you know exactly what we mean. You've seen the anticipation—and then the joy—on the faces of children as they eagerly open a birthday gift. As a result, you too experienced joy!

Well, we guarantee that you—as a servant leader—will experience the same level of joy as you watch those you serve unwrap the gifts you give them. Whether it's a smile, or a tender touch, or a little slice of hope—it doesn't matter. What matters most is that you gave, and someone else received. That you opened your heart, and another person opened his or her heart in return.

This is the reality of servant leadership. Better than that, it's also the *joy* and the *reward*.

Servant leadership will take you on an amazing journey. Get ready for the ride of your life!

—RICH AND ROBYN WILKERSON

CHAPTER ONE

SQUARE ONE

"One thing I know; the only ones among you who will be really happy are those who will have sought and found how to serve."

—ALBERT SCHWEITZER
(GERMAN-FRENCH THEOLOGIAN/
PHILOSOPHER/PHYSICIAN, 1875-1965)

WE HOPE THAT ALL OF YOU reading this book have, at some point in your lives, volunteered to serve some important cause. Have you ever done any of the following?

- Run a marathon or half-marathon (or walked or bicycled) to raise money for cancer or diabetes or AIDS?

- Donated a bag of groceries to a community food shelf?

- Served a meal at a homeless shelter?

- Tutored a young student through The Boys and Girls Clubs?

- Coached a Little League team—or soccer or basketball?

- Taught Sunday school or Hebrew school at your place of worship?

- Served as a classroom aide or done a presentation on Career Day at your child's school?

- Helped organize a chapter of Junior Achievement?

- Cleaned up a city park or helped make repairs on a home owned by an elderly citizen—perhaps as part of a service organization such as Rotary International?

- Walked the Block to distribute information on behalf of a particular candidate for political office?

- Participated in a Neighborhood Watch program?

- Said yes when a Girl Scout asked you to buy cookies? (We admit our family has always had a weakness for those peanut butter patties they call Tagalongs!)

All of these acts of volunteerism are among the many ways you can become engaged in bettering your community. They are some of the things you *should* do, in alignment with your own principles, beliefs, and goals.

The world needs volunteers. But how do these beneficial acts differ from servant leadership? In order to answer that question, we have to begin by asking the four essential questions this book will seek to answer:

1. What is a servant leader?

2. What are the characteristics of a servant leader?

3. What does a servant leader do?

4. How do you become a servant leader?

And an even more basic question:

5. Why would you want to be a servant leader?

These questions—and their answers—are the "1-2-3," the "A-B-C," and the "Do-Re-Mi" of the entire topic. They are much like the essentials from which math springs, from which literature is created, and from which music is born.

With that, the ride begins! We hope you'll join us, stay with us, and enjoy the adventure!

WHAT IS A SERVANT LEADER?

Many people—including the authors of several bestselling books on the subject—have offered their thoughts on what a servant leader is and what a servant leader does.

Our definition is simple and straightforward. A servant leader is someone who cares about the needs of others as much as, or more than, their own needs, who focuses their attention on the goals that make the world a better place, and who speaks out and acts on behalf of those who may not be able to speak for or fully represent themselves through their own actions. A servant leader does this without thought of fame, fortune, or personal gain of any kind. A servant leader never tries to accumulate riches at the

> **Servant leadership is the most satisfying and fulfilling way to live, because you are serving others and in the process improving yourself.**

expense of others, or get elected to high office simply to obtain all the power or perks associated with that position.

Above all, a servant leader is someone who is in the unique position to do something that no one else (or, at least, few others) can do. And they do it willingly. Servant leadership is a "self-inflicted accountability in the service of others."[1] Servant leadership is the most satisfying and fulfilling way to live, because you are serving others and in the process improving yourself.

In an interview with the *New York Times,* world renowned physician and global health expert Dr. Paul Farmer reflected on servant leadership, stating, "For me, it's an area of moral clarity. You're in front of someone who's suffering and you have the tools at your disposal to alleviate that suffering or even eradicate it, and you act."[2] Dr. Farmer articulates what we believe is at the core of servant leadership, utilizing all resources at our disposal to help others.

Now, before you break out in a sweat and put this book on a shelf next to the other books you've quit reading before page thirty (we've all done that—admit it!), we want to assure you we're not going to ask you to take a bullet for anyone. You aren't required to die for someone after reading this book. On the contrary, after reading this book, you just may decide to *live* like you've never lived before!

We enjoy reading the Bible together as a couple and discussing what we read. One of our favorite scriptures, one we feel is a nearly perfect description—from more than two millennia ago—describes the impact a servant leader has on those they serve:

I was hungry and you fed me,
I was thirsty and you gave me a drink,
I was homeless and you gave me a room,
I was shivering and you gave me clothes,
I was sick and you stopped to visit,
I was in prison and you came to me.[3]

As simple as it sounds, we believe true servant leaders of today follow this model. We realize that this may not be very appealing to some of our readers right at this moment. Many readers may not want to hand money or food to a transient, or serve a meal at a homeless shelter, or stop by a hospital, or visit someone who is incarcerated in a prison.

But don't tune us out just yet! There are countless ways beyond these basics in which you can serve. All of them are significant. In the pages that follow, we will introduce you to special people and tell you about the amazing things they have done...most of them without ever visiting a prison or giving their coat or a bottle of water to a stranger.

WHAT ARE THE CHARACTERISTICS
OF A SERVANT LEADER?

We believe a servant leader has the right *attitude*, the right *motivation*, and the right *resiliency* to make significant things happen. Servant leaders approach the things they believe they should do with humility, much like Mother Teresa. They believe in the reasons they desire to serve, and they "stick to it." We define these qualities as traits. All of them are important, and we'll look at them in the pages ahead.

WHAT DOES A SERVANT LEADER DO?

In looking at servant leaders from thousands of years ago to today, it seems to us that all of them do one or more (or even all) of the following:

- They respond to needs. They fill voids.
- They form partnerships or teams to meet those needs.
- They support, inspire, and manage those teams.
- If they are people of faith, they often pray.

HOW DO YOU BECOME A SERVANT LEADER?

The answer may be far more basic than you might guess. Very simply, you open your mind, your eyes, and your heart. You open your mind to the possibility of serving others, you open your eyes in order to see the opportunities for service that surround you, and you open your heart to the needs of individuals within your sphere of influence. Charles Dickens once famously penned, "No one is useless in this world who lightens the burdens of another."[4] Dickens brilliantly captured the essence and value of serving others, for it is in serving others that one finds true value and significance.

Not long ago, during one of our team gatherings, one of our Freedom School instructors asked if he could speak. We gave Jack Petion the microphone so he could address the sixty staff members who meet every Monday morning to help launch the activities of the week at Trinity Miami.

Jack gave an incredible presentation in which he recounted something that had happened the previous Friday. Here are the basics of the story. "Last Friday, Vlad (Vlad Joseph-Octave is also on our team as an AmeriCorps member) and I were in the car. I was driving when all of a sudden Vlad screamed out, 'Oh, look out!'

"I looked to my right and everything went into slow motion from that point on. We watched as a car flipped over onto its roof and lay there in traffic. By now, I had slowed down. Before I knew what was happening, Vlad had jumped out of our moving vehicle and was racing over a median, weaving in and out of traffic. I quickly pulled the car around the block and came up behind the accident to see Vlad pulling two people out of the car. They were bleeding profusely all over his clothes and he was saying, 'Are you alright? We're here for you . . . whatever you need, we're not leaving.'

"Very shortly thereafter, police officers and EMT workers in ambulances arrived, and the victims, though somewhat mangled, will live.

> **It is in serving others that one finds true value and significance.**

"As I was thinking about the event over the weekend, it occurred to me that I was raised in a culture that doesn't help anybody! Vlad is one of my best friends, and we've both been a part of Trinity for a couple of years. I can see how the culture of this place and the attitude of servant leadership has changed our lives. There was no discussion as to whether or not we would help, whether we would get blood on our clothes, or whether or not we were the right people for the job. No, it's what we do. It's who we are."

In that moment, as we heard this six-foot, six-inch, handsome Haitian tell the story, we thought to ourselves, Trinity Miami is not so much a location as it is an idea.

The idea is that wherever we go, the attitude of servant leadership follows. That's true of all of us, no matter if we're in Miami, Sioux Falls, Lubbock, or Tacoma.

We have the shared idea that we are people of respect, we are people of service, and we are people of blessing. So it's really not about us—it's about the ideas and ideals we share. The more we can multiply our ideals, the more healing we can bring to our hurting communities. John Maxwell, highly acclaimed author and leadership consultant, once wrote, "A leader knows the way, goes the way, and shows the way."[5] The true test of servant leadership isn't simply your ability to articulate ideas and ideals, nor is it simply your ability to exhibit those ideas and ideals in your life. The true test of leadership is to inspire those you lead to replicate those ideas and ideals in their own service to others.

According to J. T. Whetstone, the servant leader must abandon preconceptions of "how best to serve, then wait and listen until others define their own needs and can state them clearly. A leader builds people through service when he genuinely puts people first, viewing them as humans worthy of dignity and respect."[6]

Jack's story about the accident illustrates that what servant leadership does *not* require is special training. No college degree is required. True, certain specialized skills may be of benefit in certain situations, but the one skill common to all servant leaders is *breathing*. If you're alive, there's something you can do. In fact, you might just be amazed by how ordinary and average some of the leaders we introduce to you really are.

As you read this book, our hope is that one thought will pop into your mind again and again: "I can do this!"

REFLECTION QUESTIONS

1. As you read our definition of a servant leader, can you think of servant leaders in your life? What qualities/actions do they have that you would like to incorporate into your own role as a servant leader?

2. What do you do as a servant leader? How do you respond to needs, form partnerships, and support, inspire, and manage others?

3. Think back to situations when you had the opportunity to be a servant leader. Did you take that opportunity? If so, how has it changed your life? If not, what was holding you back? Have you made changes that will allow you to move forward as a servant leader?

ACTION SUGGESTION

Find a servant leader you know and thank them for making the decision to lead by serving others. Ask them what qualities they think have made them an effective servant leader.

CHAPTER TWO

THE "WHO" OF SERVANT LEADERSHIP

"Servant-leadership is all about making the goals clear and then rolling your sleeves up and doing whatever it takes to help people win. In that situation, they don't work for you, you work for them."

—KEN BLANCHARD

SERVANT LEADERS HAVE ONE THING in common. They have a "heart" for serving others. They have a desire to make a difference, to change the world for the better—even if only in small ways no one else notices. After all, servant leadership isn't an act or a performance staged to impress others.

According to former CEO of International Telephone and Telegraph Corporation, Harold Geeney, "Leadership is practiced not so much in words as in attitudes and actions."[1] There is no pedigree or profile of a leader; rather, we believe leadership is a set of innate qualities that manifest themselves in the attitudes and actions of ordinary people who become extraordinary.

Other than their desire to make a difference, they have little or nothing in common with one another. They don't look a certain way, dress a certain way, or act a certain way. They don't eat the same food, play the same sports, enjoy the same movies, or listen to the same music. Some servant leaders listen to rap or hip-hop, others attend the opera. For others still, it's good old country or reggae. It is, in fact, their diversity—and their individuality—that make them both special and significant.

As we explore the following list of who servant leaders are, we want you to realize we know at least one person who fits every single category, and we'll do our best to tell you some of their true stories.

We don't know about you, but we've always learned the best lessons from simple stories, and we've passed those lessons on to our four sons. Here are some examples:

- From *The Three Little Pigs*, we've taught them that we should always build for our future with the strongest materials we can find. So we've tried to build our lives—and the lives of our children—out of bricks rather than straw.

- From *Little Red Riding Hood*, we learned that things aren't always as they appear, so it often pays to question what "seems to be."

- From *The Lion King*—a story our family has watched together more than once—we learned that it's important to prepare future generations for leadership, because they are certain to inherit our world one day.

So, to most effectively share our thoughts on servant leadership, we're going to tell the stories of some very special people who, at the same time, are often very ordinary people. We believe these individuals embody the principle one of the nation's most revered servant leaders, Dr. Martin Luther King Jr., articulated in his 1968 sermon "The Drum Major Instinct":

> Everybody can be great, because everybody can serve. You don't have to have a college degree to serve. You don't have to make your subject and verb agree to serve. You only need a heart full of grace. A soul generated by love.[2]

You see, there really is no such thing as a typical servant leader. The stereotypes simply don't apply. Servant leaders can be any age, male or female, any race, any nationality, any religion or creed, any socio-economic standing, any educational background.

ANY AGE

We have all watched as preteens—even children who are only seven, eight, or nine years old—have identified needs and taken action to meet those needs. You've probably read or seen news reports about children who hold car washes or operate lemonade stands to raise money for other children with serious illnesses, or those who gave their holiday gifts to families who lost their homes to fires, floods, hurricanes, or tornadoes. Seven-year-old Charlie Simpson, from west London, is an amazing example of the generosity of children. He raised $240,000 for the Haiti earthquake victims, at seven years old![3] Children do these things not to gain recognition, but because there are huge servant hearts beating inside those small bodies.

A young man from our church, Eric Quinn, is a wonderful example of someone who developed a heart for serving at a young age.

When Eric was just two years old his dad left the family, and he never saw him again. Eric's older brother Travis, who was only six at the time, became his protector. Travis also looked out for their older sister, Latasha, who was ten.

Travis and Latasha turned out to be outstanding students who were also musically gifted. Eric, on the other hand, was not much into school, at least not in his early years. But he was very into his older brother.

> **"**
> Servant leaders can be any age, male or female, any race, any nationality, any religion or creed, any socio-economic standing, any educational background.

In his early teen years, Travis connected with the African Heritage Cultural Center, running the lights and sound for several stage productions and other public events. He developed a genuine gift in this area.

Eric tagged along with his older brother. Even though only seven at the time, he was as fascinated by the art and technology of lighting as Travis was, so they worked side-by-side at the Cultural Center.

When Eric visited Trinity Church for the first time at age thirteen, he was immediately impressed by the fact that we employed so-called intelligent lighting. This means the lights can be computer programmed to operate in coordination with the events taking place during the program. The thing is, it takes a brilliant individual to operate this complex system.

Eric turned out to be that person. Other leaders in the church often commented to us that Eric practically lived on our campus— he was that involved. We had to reassure his mother he was okay.

Here was a young man living inside a junior-high body but possessing technical skills far beyond his years. He was brilliant! The staff at the African Heritage Cultural Center recognized Eric's talents, so they offered him a job. In fact, he became so well known that he was asked to create the lighting for major shows in the largest venues around South Florida. But that didn't stop him from serving at Trinity.

Life changed for Eric in October of 2012. We were doing a large show at the church called "The Voice and the Judgment." The seven performances involved a cast of sixty actors and a crew of 150. It was a huge endeavor, and Eric was in charge of lighting.

Eric was at a bus stop on Highway 441, about two miles from church, at 4:00 in the afternoon. He was on his way to direct lighting for the 7:00 p.m. performance. As he waited for the bus, the driver of a speeding car lost control, slammed into another car, went airborne, flipped over, and landed on Eric and others waiting for the bus.

One woman was killed, another woman had to have both legs amputated, and a third woman lost an arm and a leg. Eric was pinned under the car and, in desperation, instinctively tried to push the car off his body. He grabbed the hot exhaust pipe in the process, and severely burned his hands.

He screamed for help, but no one was nearby. Finally, two teenagers, Austin and Justin Hines, and a man from a neighboring barbershop somehow lifted the car up and pulled Eric to safety. He was airlifted to the Trauma Center in Hollywood, Florida, where it was determined that he had a crushed pelvis, a crushed right leg, and a severely damaged main artery—on top of the burns he suffered. He endured eight grueling surgeries over the next several months, and for a time it seemed certain he would lose his leg.

> **"**
> There are endless settings and situations where the leadership of women is both more appropriate, and more effective, than that of men.

We had faith he would recover and once again assume his servant leadership role. As a sort of "We love you and we're with you, Eric" gift, we bought him the latest iPad. Most of his life, he had gotten few gifts, so we could tell he truly appreciated it.

Today, Eric's burned hands have no scars. Although he still walks with a limp, thanks to intensive physical therapy, he experiences little pain.

Eric's older brother, Travis, stopped in to see us recently. He said, "You know that iPad you gave Eric? He's already created an App that will allow him to control all of the church's lighting from the palm of his hand."

Despite all he's been through—and although he has not yet turned seventeen—Eric is the embodiment of a simple truth:

Those who have the heart of servant leaders will always be servant leaders—and they won't let setbacks or their age stop them. In his book, *Fresh Air,* Christian leader Chris Hodges states, "If we want to enjoy a vibrant, fully alive life, we must have something to focus on that is bigger than our problems."[4] What Eric's story demonstrates is that the willingness and desire to serve others, in spite of personal hardships and pains, is the only way to live a fulfilled and purposeful life. As you will learn, this is the true fountain of youth.

As young as some budding servant leaders are, others are nearing the end of their lives. They may have been opening their hearts to others for decades, or they may have discovered the beauty of servant leadership after they retired. Later on, we'll tell the story of O. A. Alderson, who served others until the day he died.

The point is, age—lack of it or "too much" of it—is no excuse for inaction.

MALE OR FEMALE

This one needs even less explanation than the "age" category. In most of the world, equality of the sexes is both an accepted and a revered point of view. True, there are cultures where women are still denied equal status, but even in those cultures, women have found opportunities to boldly and bravely serve others—even if they can't serve openly. So, women, don't let "I'm just a stay-at-home mom" stand in your way. Realize that there are endless settings and situations where the leadership of women is both more appropriate, and more effective, than that of men.

ANY RACE

When Rich was a child, he became acutely aware of the struggles of African-Americans in the U.S., and the leadership mantle that Dr. Martin Luther King, Jr., had assumed. This, despite the fact that he didn't live in the U.S. at the time.

Here's Rich's story in his own words:

My earliest recollection in life was when I was a little over three years of age, living in the Bahamas. Everyone in my world was black. My black friends stayed at my house or I overnighted at theirs. Our parents were always hanging out together.

One day, I asked my mother, "Why doesn't God like us?"

"What do you mean?"

"Everyone else is black and we're not."

She replied, "Richie, you know God loves all colors."

I looked at her and said, "I know, mom, but we don't have any color at all. We're white."

As a result of my upbringing, it's difficult for me to comprehend racism. In fact I had to come back to America to learn about racism. It simply didn't exist in my family in the Bahamas.

Every person, no matter what race they are, can become a servant leader.

ANY NATIONALITY

Economists, politicians, and the media sometimes try to divide the world on the basis of the "haves" and the "have-nots." They talk about third-world countries and emerging cultures and so on. The reality is that every nation of the world can boast about amazing servant leaders. They may not necessarily have money, or position, or great power, but they have what it takes to make a difference—a servant's heart. Mother Teresa[5] and Mahatma Ghandi[6] are well-known examples of servant leaders from other nations.

ANY RELIGION OR CREED

History is heavy-laden with examples of people doing despicable things in the name of religion, even though it seems it has never really mattered which religion. There are innumerable events in the past that should compel all of us, of every faith, to beg for forgiveness from our fellow man. Slavery in the United States and in other countries, as well as atrocities and acts of genocide around the world, has given religion a very bad name.

Fortunately, real faith and genuine practice are far different than religion. Those who observe the deeply revered tenets of most of the world's religions practice love, compassion, and servant leadership, and abhor the "religion of hate."

Those who observe the deeply revered tenets of most of the world's religions practice love, compassion, and servant leadership, and abhor the "religion of hate."

You may be Jewish, Christian, Muslim, Sikh, Hindu, Buddhist, an agnostic, a confirmed atheist, "something else" or "none of the above"—it doesn't matter. You have a vital role to play in serving others.

ANY SOCIO/ECONOMIC STANDING

We could tell you countless stories about the rich and powerful who are struck with the notion of serving others. And you might say, "Well, they *should* be. They have the money, and they probably have the time." Our experience, however, is that those who aren't rich and powerful often emerge as the true leaders. They are the unsung heroes among us.

Can you imagine a man who many of us would think of as poor starting a small but effective organization in Southern California to serve meals to the homeless? We know of that man through a friend, and his story is inspiring.

Can you imagine another man in prison in Arizona—one serving a life sentence for a series of nonviolent crimes—who has become a servant leader and a model prisoner? He works in the prison library for thirty-five cents an hour, and volunteers to teach prisoners. He then uses his meager earnings to organize fundraisers to help the struggling wives of other prisoners. He and the other men whose help he enlisted recently sold $11,000 of pizzas to the other inmates, and raised $4,000 for his charity.

If men and women have a heart for servant leadership, their social or economic standing—or lack of it—won't stop them.

ANY EDUCATIONAL BACKGROUND

There was a time in the past when the circumstances of life often dictated that women didn't receive much education because they had to forego school to help raise their siblings, or that men dropped out of school by sixth grade to help on the family farm. Yet history shows many of them still became leaders who served others capably.

These days, more of us than ever before graduate from high school, go on to college, or complete a post-graduate degree program. But if we were to make the mistake of abdicating leadership roles to those with the most education, our world would be in sorry shape.

Often, people discredit themselves from becoming extraordinary simply because they don't feel qualified; however, we wholeheartedly believe that what is required of a servant leader is simply a desire to serve and a willingness to be used by God. In his book *Run with the Horses,* Eugene Peterson brilliantly captures this thought: "It is not our feelings that determine our level of participation in life, nor our experience that qualifies us for what we will do and be; it is what God decides about us. God does not send us into the dangerous and exacting life of faith because we are qualified; he chooses us in order to qualify us for what he wants us to be and do."[6] No one with a servant's heart should ever sideline themselves because of a lack of education. There are too many significant things to accomplish! Everyone needs to be in the game.

Now that we know the "who" of servant leadership—everyone, including you—the remaining chapters of this book will focus primarily on the traits of the servant leader. These are the qualities that have nothing to do with your skills, abilities, and talents, and everything to do with the person you are, the person you want to be, and the person you are willing to become.

Ordinary, everyday people all over the world are becoming extraordinary leaders—because they are willing to serve others.

REFLECTION QUESTIONS

1. Have you encountered unexpected servant leaders in your life? Children, those past retirement age, or someone from disadvantaged circumstances?

2. Think about Eric's story. Here is a young man who has lived through so much in his young life, and still has a passion for serving others. Do you have that passion in your life? How do you show it?

3. Have you ever sidelined yourself because you thought you didn't have "what it takes," be it education, social standing, or age and experience?

ACTION SUGGESTION

Consider one small thing you can do to serve someone else, and make a point to do it.

CHAPTER THREE

THE TRAITS OF A SERVANT LEADER

—

"There are no greater treasures than the highest human qualities such as compassion, courage and hope. Not even tragic accident or disaster can destroy such treasures of the heart."

—DAISAKU IKEDA
(EDUCATOR, BUDDHIST PHILOSOPHER, AND PEACEBUILDER)

THE DICTIONARY DEFINES *trait* as "a distinguishing quality or characteristic as of personality."[1] *Visual Thesaurus* defines it as "a distinguishing feature of your personal nature."[2] If you were to type t-r-a-i-t into *Visual Thesaurus*, you would see dozens of descriptive words. Among them: *emotionlessness, frivolousness, distrustfulness, thoughtlessness, compulsiveness,* and many other not-so-positive descriptions of human nature.

But you would also find many positive words: *humbleness, resoluteness, trustworthiness, thoughtfulness, faithfulness,* and other positive descriptions of our natures. Servant leaders invariably exhibit humanity's most positive traits. They build their lives around those traits, and they put the person they are into action. Their authenticity, being true to who they are, exists no matter what role they take.[3]

There's no way we could possibly list all the traits of an effective servant leader. Some of them are as simple as "listening." But here are the fifteen traits we believe are the most vital to any servant who wants to lead others toward positive change.

- They have a clear vision.
- They have absolute values.
- They are faithful.
- They are accepting.
- They are loyal.
- They are humble.
- They have integrity.
- They are compassionate.
- They are encouragers. They support one another.
- They are generous.
- They honor and respect one another. They value the contributions of others.
- They mentor one another.
- They are flexible.

- They "bounce back"—they are resilient, and they help others to bounce back.

- They are selfless. They are willing to give it their all.

You probably expected us to include "They love others" on our list. The fact is, we believe most of the traits we've listed are key manifestations of love: faithfulness, acceptance, compassion, encouragement, generosity, and selflessness among them. Even integrity, humility, mentoring, accountability, and resilience can be part of the overall package we call love.

You might also have expected us to include skills, abilities, or talents somewhere in the list. But skills, abilities, and talents are different from traits. We refer to these three things as gifts. It's your job to unwrap them.

You may have the ability to teach—the gift of teaching—but if you aren't teaching, you aren't serving others with that ability. You may be a skilled carpenter, mechanic, or pilot, but if you're not building to serve others, doing car repairs for nothing more than money, or flying a plane without providing acts of service to others, you aren't using your gifts. Your traits are what empower you to apply your gifts . . . to make them more significant by serving others.

Traits may be inherent in some individuals, or they may be the outcome of environment—good parents or schools, for example. For the most part, though, we

> Traits are the motivation behind the gifts—behind the skills, abilities, and talents, behind the behaviors and attitudes generally present in all servant leaders.

believe they are cultivated out of personal desire. If we want to be generous, we'll find a way. If we want to encourage others, we'll make it happen. If we want to mentor others, we'll take the time.

Traits are the motivation behind the gifts—behind the skills, abilities, and talents, behind the behaviors and attitudes generally present in all servant leaders.[4] Let's explore those traits together.

REFLECTION QUESTIONS

1. Consider the fifteen traits we give for a servant leader. Now take a few minutes to consider how these traits fit into your life. Be honest with yourself: not everyone will have every trait right at the start. Which do you already possess? Which do you need to develop?

2. Are you using the traits you possess to serve others? If not, why? What can you do to change this? If you are using them, are you using them in the capacity of a servant leader?

3. Selflessness is a difficult trait to cultivate. Our natural nature demands we put our survival before others, and that tends to bleed over to other parts of our lives. Can you think of ways you have been selfless in the past week, month, year?

ACTION SUGGESTION

Pick one trait you feel you need to work on. For the next week, be intentional about cultivating that trait within yourself at least once a day. If you want to go further, do it for twenty-one days. According to some experts, twenty-one days of repetition can lead to permanent acceptance of an action/thought pattern!

CHAPTER FOUR

VISION

———

"The only thing worse than being blind is having sight but no vision."
—HELEN KELLER

THERE ARE PEOPLE WALKING among us—people you know well—who wander through life with no purpose, without direction, completely devoid of vision. The fact that you are reading this book clearly indicates you are not among them. Chances are, you even have a list of written goals for your life and your vision is clear.

Vision evolves during life. It's moving, it's dynamic, it's ever-changing. How many young boys do we all know who want to be police officers, or firefighters, or NBA or NFL stars? They look at girls their age and say "yuck." But they become teachers, chemists, real estate agents, accountants, mechanics, carpenters, or pilots. They also become husbands, fathers, and, yes, servant leaders.

How many young girls do we know who want to become nurses, or NASCAR drivers, or astronauts, or lawyers, or actresses, or mommies? And then they become those things! Or they become senators or governors . . . and mommies, too. Above all, they grow from girls into women, and they become servant leaders.

What we are saying—on a basic level—is that what you once wanted to be, and what you have ultimately become, are both outcomes of your vision for your life. They may actually be one and the same, but they are, nonetheless, the product of your vision.

When you were a child, your vision likely didn't include anything about servant leadership. The fact is, all of us, as children, were concentrating on "me, me, me."

It's important that the servant leader have a vision large enough to include the needs and empowerment of others, but also well-defined enough to inspire others to follow. In their book, *The Servant Leader,* Ken Blanchard and Phil Hodges discuss the importance of a servant leader's vision stating, "Servant leadership begins with a clear and compelling vision of the future that excites passion in the leader and commitment in those who follow."[1] It's only when we grow up and recognize that the world is a seriously needy place, that we begin to consider the significance of a vision that incorporates servant leadership.

The question then becomes, "How do you determine your vision and how do you pursue it?"

WRITE DOWN YOUR VISION

You don't need to express your vision in eloquent words, lofty phrases, or precise terms. You can write your vision on a scrap of paper. You can write it on a napkin from Chick-fil-A or

McDonalds. You can write it on the back side of a letter from your mother. The key point is that you write your vision down on something and keep it. You might even want to buy a $3.00 frame and hang it on your wall.

We have a friend who was forced, mostly against his will, to write a term paper in high school about what he wanted to do in his life. It was a career class, and he was asked to choose a career path and write about it. He essentially pulled a needle out of a haystack and decided that he wanted to go to college, study journalism, advertising, and public relations, and then start his own business—one to help market nonprofits.

Without fully realizing it, he had developed his vision, had written it down, and was about to embark on a path to achieve it. He enrolled at the University of Minnesota, completed his degree, worked for a couple of nonprofit organizations while in school, and upon graduation, started the company he had envisioned, and then operated it for more than twenty-three years. One of the nonprofits he worked for while in college became his first client.

> **"**
>
> Your vision can actually become integral to your character as a servant leader.

God spoke to Habakkuk, a prophet to the nation of Israel, about the importance of writing down a vision. In Habakkuk 2:3–5, God instructs Habakkuk saying, "Write this. Write what you see. Write it out in big block letters so that it can be read on the run. This vision-message is a witness pointing to what's coming. It aches for the coming—it can hardly wait! And it doesn't lie. If it seems slow in coming, wait. It's on its way. It will come right on time." Writing down a vision helps focus and articulate a dream; it gives the servant leader a tangible outcome to work towards.

Words have power. If you haven't read Joel Osteen's book, *I Declare*, we strongly recommend you do. Joel reveals the power that your declarations can have, and he demonstrates how your vision impacts your life. Your vision can actually become integral to your character as a servant leader.[2]

SHARE YOUR VISION

A key component of a servant leader's vision is the ability to coalesce a team that will help that vision come to fruition. In order to effectively lead a team, a leader must be able to identify and articulate a specific vision. In *The Leadership Challenge,* coauthors James Kouzes and Barry Posner reinforce this principle saying, "Leaders have to make sure that what they see is also something that others can see. When visions are shared they attract more people, sustain higher levels of motivation, and withstand more challenges than those that are singular."[3] A servant leader who can not only cast a vision but share that vision with others, will further the impact they have in serving others.

Several years ago, we had a dinnertime conversation about our individual visions for our lives. We came to the conclusion that because we are a married couple we needed to share our vision. We decided our hearts truly belonged to people who needed God's love, and we needed to be the hands and feet to bring it to them.

As a result, we came to Miami to lead a group of people called Trinity Church. At that time, there were about 250 to 300 people in the church—mostly of Haitian heritage. Other nationalities and people would join us from time to time, but our core group was—and is—primarily Haitian.

The area of the city we came to was North Miami. Most of the people were disenfranchised members of society. We were surrounded by poverty, pain, and serious need. We can't really explain why, but this seemed to be the place we were compelled to go.

We both believed we could practice servant leadership in Florida. We moved from the far northwest—the Seattle/Tacoma area—to the far southeast corner of the United States: Miami. We couldn't have put more miles between ourselves and our families if we had tried. But it was an open door, and it seemed to be the right open door for us. The move was compatible with our vision.

When we arrived in Miami, we didn't know anyone. We didn't have a doctor. We didn't even know anyone else who had a doctor. We didn't have a lawyer. We didn't have an insurance agent. We didn't know a real estate agent. We were like pioneers in a new land. But from the very first day we began to know and love the people in this church.

Now there are over 4,000 people who attend Trinity each weekend. We love them dearly. We have their backs and they have ours. Our shared vision has connected us with the most amazing, caring, sacrificial servant leaders—and true servants—on this earth.

As leaders, we wholeheartedly believe in the importance of cultivating a vision birthed out of the community in which we serve. We understand the importance of casting a vision that is not only accepted by but is encompassing of those we lead. Warren Bennis and Burt Nanus, experts in organizational leadership, discuss the importance of shared vision in their book *Leaders:*

Historians tend to write about great leaders as if they possessed transcendent genius, as if they were capable of creating their visions and sense of destiny out of some mysterious inner resource. Perhaps some do, but upon closer examination it usually turns out that the vision did not originate with the leader personally but rather from others.[4]

An effective servant leader will have a vision that is shared and developed by those whom they lead, because the leader's vision ultimately is to empower others.

YOUR VISION CAN CHANGE

Your personal vision can begin at a very early age. As we mentioned earlier, there are actually people walking among us who have no vision, but there are also those who envisioned becoming police officers, fire fighters, teachers, medical professionals, (and anything and everything else) at age six, eight, or ten. And they became what they envisioned. There are others who don't fully capture their vision until late in life. Other people begin their careers with one vision but then, for one reason or another, discover and unleash another vision.

We told you about our friend who first stated his vision way back in 1965 when he wrote a paper about how he wanted to get a college degree in advertising and public relations, and how he wanted to start a company that would help nonprofit organizations more effectively market their programs to a broader audience. He followed his vision to the letter and did exactly what he dreamed he should do.

For more than twenty years, his company capably served a variety of organizations. But in the early 1990s, the economy dealt his company a deadly blow. He lost nearly a million dollars and closed his doors. Despite this huge "hit," he refused to declare bankruptcy. It took him years to pay off his debt, but he did it.

He quickly concluded that he might be able to help others in struggling businesses get through their toughest battles, so he wrote a book about his struggles. The book was published by a major New York publisher—and that led to a "new, updated vision" for his life. He now creates books, videos, seminars, and other training materials to help people deal with their challenges in business and in life. He's currently pursuing his new vision with all his heart!

This story highlights an important principle in the vision of servant leaders: It will grow and expand as it includes the needs of others. In his book *Greater*, Steven Furtick articulates this notion declaring, "God will often launch a vision that is larger than life by bringing a person to a starting point that is small and seemingly insignificant."[5] Over the course of time, servant leaders will accomplish more than expected as they continue to serve others; their vision will grow and, as a result, their impact will grow.

> "
> Over the course of time, servant leaders will accomplish more than expected as they continue to serve others; their vision will grow and, as a result, their impact will grow.

FROM NIGHT TO DAY

One of the most dramatic examples of how someone's vision can change is the story of a historical figure named Saul of Tarsus. If you think that doesn't sound like a current name—even for a rapper—you're right.

Saul was a really religious guy who lived during the time of Jesus. He was a guy who decided his goal should be to persecute those who believed in a man many claimed had risen from the dead after being crucified. And by persecute, we mean maim, dismember, and kill.

That was his vision. But his vision changed the day he had an actual vision. He was blinded by a bright light that was a vision of Christ, who asked him, "Saul, why do you persecute me?"

Saul didn't have a good answer to that question, but a strange "other-world sighting" resulted in his total blindness. He was led to a house in a nearby city where his vision was miraculously restored.

That's when the vision for his life was transformed from persecuting believers in Christ to spreading the story of Jesus throughout the known world. He became known as Paul, and he went from persecutor to being persecuted himself. He became a servant leader who endured horrific shipwrecks and years of imprisonment for his new cause—his new vision. Paul models the vision of a servant leader who "lives, loves and leads by conscience—the inward moral sense of what is right and what is wrong."[6] When God showed Paul the path of right, Paul allowed his conscience and his belief in what was right to change his vision. His vision changed so much, he was responsible for writing the majority of the books in the New Testament of the Bible.

The keys to vision are simple and clear:

- Determine your vision.

- Write it down—state it clearly.

- Share it. Spread your vision to others. That will make it bigger and give it greater impact.

- Be willing to allow your vision to change. People grow . . . and so does their vision. You don't know what the future will bring into your life. But you can always know one thing: your vision and your impact as a servant leader can—and will—change the world!

REFLECTION QUESTIONS

1. Do you have a well-defined vision for your life? Have you written it down? Does it include the needs and empowerment of others?

2. Has a servant leader in your life ever shared their vision with you? If so, were you inspired by that vision? Have you shared your vision with others?

3. Have circumstances in your life caused your vision to change? Consider for a moment how your vision enriches your life and the lives of those around you. If it has changed, how has it affected not only you, but those around you?

ACTION SUGGESTION

Write your vision down! Even if you have a vision written down, re-write it. Spend a few moments each day for the next week considering the words and how they impact your life and the lives of those you lead. Share your vision with them!

CHAPTER FIVE

VALUES

"If we are to go forward, we must go back and rediscover those precious values—that all reality hinges on moral foundations and that all reality has spiritual control."
—MARTIN LUTHER KING, JR.

VALUES IMPACT OUR LIVES and our effectiveness as servant leaders in three ways:

- First, our values influence our decisions.
- Second, they motivate our actions.
- Third, they affect the way we treat other people.

It's important to note that nations, individuals, and organizations are all guided by their values.

For example, the Declaration of Independence is a clear statement of the values that guided the formation of the United States of America: "We hold these truths to be self-evident, that all men are created equal, that they are endowed by their Creator with certain unalienable rights, that among these are life, liberty and the pursuit of happiness."

Our nation's founders valued equality and human rights—although it took a century to grant freedom to slaves, and even longer to make true equality a reality for millions of Americans. Among the rights our founders valued are life, liberty, and the pursuit of happiness. Values don't get more basic than that!

Likewise, organizations (including companies, nonprofits, and educational institutions) are guided by values that are generally clearly stated.

One organization that has received much acclaim for their values, and as a result has experienced great operational success, is Chick-fil-A. In an industry that celebrates speed and efficiency, Chick-fil-A demonstrates that remaining steadfast in values and principles as an organization doesn't necessarily come at the expense of profit margins. One such example is the emphasis and value placed on exceptional customer service, which is an intrinsic value possessed by every member of the Chick-fil-A organization. In a recent article in *Fast Company,* writer Chuck Salter discussed the origin of this value system: "President and chief operating officer Dan Cathy infuses everyone from franchise owner-operators to teenagers earning $9 an hour with his passion for service and his conviction in its intrinsic worth—to the individual as well as the company."[1] Dan Cathy and the Chick-fil-A Corporation exemplify the importance of infusing all members of an organization or team with shared values and convictions.

As individuals, our values are likely as diverse as we are. We value everything from family to faith, from friendships to freedom, from education to health and physical fitness. "Values are the foundations of our opinions, preferences, choices, and decisions. We cannot and do not make value-free decisions. When a choice is difficult, we need clarity about what matters, to us and to others."[2] Our belief is that there are two basic categories of individual values—superficial and sacrificial.

Superficial values include such things as appearance (clothing, hair, makeup, etc.), fame, power (especially over others), and outward signs of success (cars, big homes, boats, exotic vacations). Please understand that we're not saying there is anything necessarily wrong with looking your best, dressing well, or driving a nice car. But if these things are your core values—if they take over your life—you may not have enough time, energy, or money left to serve others. That's why we call these things superficial values.

In contrast, sacrificial values place the needs of others first. Being an attentive, involved, loving parent is an example of a sacrificial value. Serving a Scouting troop because you want to help mold the lives of future generations is a sacrificial value. Giving of your time, your talents, or your money—even when it may be inconvenient—is another example.

In a recent interview with Dave Ramsey, world-renowned author and public speaker Rabbi Daniel Lapin presented an illustration that not only demonstrates sacrificial value in action, but has also revolutionized our personal perspective on money and finances. When asked about negative perceptions about making money, Rabbi Lapin responded, "Imagine that I'm a roofer and your roof is leaking, and it's Sunday afternoon, and I wanted to take my kid to the zoo, but instead you call me up and say that your roof's leaking. Fine, I come fix your roof. That night I go to my wife and say, 'Listen, we didn't make the zoo so instead let's go out for a nice steak and chips dinner.' We walk into the restaurant and the restaurateur says, 'What? You want me to go into my hot kitchen and slave over a stove just so that you can have steak and chips? Well what have you done for anyone else? If I'm going to do a service for you, I want to know that you are a part of the whole system.' I reply, 'Well as it happens, I've spent the afternoon on somebody's roof, fixing their roof and stopping the rain from coming in. I did help somebody.' He says, 'Anyone can spin a yarn, can you prove that?' I say, 'Sure' and I pull out a hundred dollars out of my pocket and wave it in front of him and say, 'You see, that proves that I fixed somebody's roof.' He says, 'Hey sorry, no problem. Make yourself comfortable, I'll be back with your food in a minute.' At the end of the meal he says, 'In a week's time, I'm going to have to take my kid to the orthodontist and he's probably going to want to know that I've done something for somebody. I'd like a certificate of performance from you, proving that I served you.' I respond, 'Sure, I've got these dollar bills; how many do you want?' and he replies, 'I'll take sixty.' I give him the sixty and off he goes."[3]

> **It is imperative that servant leaders at all levels maintain a well-tuned moral compass and make their decisions as ethical as possible.**

This illustration so beautifully debunks negative connotations associated with making money. If we view the exchange of money as a reward for a particular value, added by an act of service, then making money is not something that should be frowned upon, rather it should be heralded.

If we allow our sacrificial values to be the moral compass by which we serve, then just as with making money, we will celebrate the value added to others as the reward for being a servant leader. It is imperative that servant leaders at all levels maintain a well-tuned moral compass and make their decisions as ethical as possible. Holding this high value increases their desire to see others grow and contribute.[4]

You may be wondering, "What's the difference between values and traits? They sound the same to me." Very simply, values are something you *determine*, and traits are something you *develop*. For example: You *determine* to be an attentive, involved, loving parent. So, in response to that value, you *develop* the traits of acceptance, compassion, encouragement, generosity, mentoring, and selflessness, among many others. If you're a parent, you know what we mean!

REFLECTION QUESTIONS

1. Can you think of an organization with values you admire? Do those values inspire you as an individual? Do you find yourself incorporating any of those values into your personal life and your role as a servant leader?

2. Consider superficial and sacrificial values and the differences between them. Which do you see having more of an impact on your life? Do you need to make any changes?

3. Have you ever pictured your own personal moral compass in your mind? Close your eyes and picture it in your head. It can be as elaborate or as functional as you want. Good lies solidly to the north, bad to the south. Now picture your actions for the last few days. How many of those are on the horizon to the north of you? How many are to the south?

ACTION SUGGESTION

Be conscious of your decisions for the next few days. Take time to ponder why you are making the decision, and where it falls on your moral compass. This process may take a few minutes for a big decision (deciding to confront someone who slighted you), or just a moment for a small decision (how you answer someone's question).

CHAPTER SIX

FAITHFULNESS

"It is better to be faithful than famous."

—THEODORE ROOSEVELT

THE TOPIC OF FAITHFULNESS is very close to our hearts! We're not about to tell you that it's the most important trait, but it's certainly right up there near the top.

Returning to the dictionary for a quick definition, Webster's says being faithful means to be "constant or loyal," and to "have or show a strong sense of duty or responsibility; conscientious." Gary Bredfeldt states the faithful person is "a trustworthy individual" and faithfulness is "foundational to effectiveness" as a leader.[1]

We believe there are four ways to demonstrate faithfulness:

1. Faithfulness to yourself
2. Faithfulness to your team

3. Faithfulness to the cause

4. Faithfulness to the outcome

FAITHFULNESS TO YOURSELF

> **An effective servant leader must be unwavering in their values and personal convictions.**

Faithfulness to yourself means the ways you find to lead and serve are in complete alignment with your personal vision, values, beliefs, and goals. Servant leaders don't do things that contradict their principles. Rather, their principles and their actions are inseparably intertwined.

In their highly celebrated book, *Execution*, authors Larry Bossidy and Ram Charan discuss the importance of leaders remaining faithful to themselves: "A solid, long term leader has an ethical frame of reference that gives her the power and energy to carry out even the most difficult assignment. This characteristic is beyond honesty or beyond integrity, beyond treating people with dignity. It's a business leadership ethic."[2]

An effective servant leader must be unwavering in their values and personal convictions.

FAITHFULNESS TO YOUR TEAM

The most effective servant leaders build teams and/or participate in team efforts. Very few people can achieve their highest goals operating on their own. No quarterback has ever won the Super Bowl without talented and dedicated running backs and receivers, a solid front line, and a great defensive squad and effective special teams.

No astronaut could have landed on the moon without the involvement of tens of thousands of scientists, engineers, and ground crew members. And teachers become more effective by having a supportive principal and adding parents to their teams.

Servant leaders inspire trust in their team "by demonstrating optimism, a firm belief in the importance of the group mission or goal, showing confidence, competence, openness to change, and granting autonomy to followers in controlling their own actions."[3] It's essential to have the support of a team, but it's imperative that a servant leader maintain and build on that support by demonstrating faithfulness to the team.

One way this is achieved is by cultivating a culture of trust between the leader and those being served. Warren Benis and Burt Nanus discuss the importance of trust in their book *Leaders*. They state, "Trust is the emotional glue that binds followers and leaders together. The accumulation of trust is a measure of the legitimacy of leadership. It cannot be mandated or purchased; it must be earned."[4]

A servant leader who demonstrates faithfulness to their team will generate trust within that team over time.

FAITHFULNESS TO THE CAUSE

True servant leaders don't place anything above the cause—not even themselves or their team. The cause is the reason for serving. It's what compels and propels the servant leader. William Booth, founder of the Salvation Army, is the embodiment of a servant leader whose passion and faithfulness to a cause created a legacy of serving others.

In his biography of Booth, *Booth the Beloved,* John Evan Smith included a quote by Booth that captures his passion for serving others:

> "While women weep, as they do now, I'll fight; while little children go hungry, as they do now, I'll fight; while men go to prison, in and out, as they do now, I'll fight; while there is a drunkard left, while there is a poor lost girl upon the streets, while there remains one dark soul without the light of God, I'll fight—I'll fight to the very end!"[5]

Booth's conviction and commitment to serving the disenfranchised in society translated into a social service organization that has served millions of individuals and endured for over a century.

Of course, the cause must be a worthy one. It must benefit as many people as time, team, and funds allow. You've probably heard the disheartening stories of charities that sound worthwhile on the surface, yet when the truth is known, very little of the money raised goes to the benefit of anyone other than the founders or leaders . . . or their cronies.

> **True servant leaders don't place anything above the cause—not even themselves or their team.**

We get excited and enthusiastic about legitimate causes. In the aftermath of any natural disaster, an endless stream of fraudulent causes springs out of seemingly nowhere. This was the case after Hurricane Sandy. That is why we were so pleased that CNN ran a positive story about Convoy of Hope (www.convoyofhope.org). Founded by Hal, Steve, and David Donaldson, this servant organization really *does* what it claims to do. Their mission statement declares they have a "driving passion to feed the world through children's feeding initiatives, community outreaches, and disaster response."[6]

The leaders of this organization not only follow through on their goals, they do it efficiently and responsibly. Only 6 percent of their income goes to fundraising, just 4 percent goes to administration, and a full 90 percent goes to the actual cause—alleviating hunger and responding to disasters. In fact, Convoy of Hope is a recipient of the prestigious Four Star Charity Award from Charity Navigator, and Convoy of Hope has been accepted as a Best of America by the Independent Charities of America. Very few charities can make that claim.

Convoy of Hope was praised on CNN's *Anderson Cooper 360* for its post-Sandy work in New Jersey. "A Missouri-based charity called Convoy of Hope is here handing out coats, blankets, food, and water. Real help for real victims."[7] Obviously this organization is faithful to the cause. They are not "in it" for themselves—they are in it for others. That's a true mark of servant leadership.

FAITHFULNESS TO THE OUTCOME

It's been said that the world is essentially divided into two basic groups: starters and finishers. Starters have great ideas and can provide the leadership to successfully initiate a venture or a cause. Finishers have the ability to see ventures, projects, or causes through to completion.

If you are a starter who cannot finish things, you must partner with a finisher to make the outcome happen. And if you are a finisher, you must partner with a starter in order to have a worthwhile cause to pursue . . . and complete.

It often takes two, to achieve an outcome. Even if you are effective at both starting and finishing, you still need a team to quickly and efficiently reach your desired outcome. The important thing is, no matter where you fall in the starting/finishing spectrum, you must be committed to the outcome!

But there's more to faithfulness! And, to us, it's very personal. As Christian leaders, we believe the Bible is not only the foundation of our faith, we wholeheartedly believe it contains valuable and insightful principles essential to any leader.

> **"**
> To us personally, faith means we are willing to accept things we cannot see or prove, and believe in the possibility of fulfilled outcomes that have not yet happened.

With that "disclaimer" behind us, we need to tell you that faithfulness often means we personally need to have faith. But what is faith?

To us personally, faith means we are willing to accept things we cannot see or prove, and believe in the possibility of fulfilled outcomes that have not yet happened. As husband and wife, we agree completely on this principle.

Here's an example. Why do millions of people participate in the Susan G. Komen Race for the Cure? Simple. They have faith that the money they raise by running and walking will one day (soon, we all hope!) result in a cure for breast cancer. They have faith that lives will be saved—the lives of their mothers, sisters, and friends, and perhaps even their own lives.

Another example: why do people give money to causes such as World Vision and Food for the Hungry—organizations that feed starving people and provide medical services to them? Very simply, they have faith that their donations will save lives and help eradicate hunger.

In these two cases (as well as many others), the participants can't actually see the outcome. They can only *visualize* the outcome. The difference between seeing and visualizing is called faith.

In his memoir, *My Journey,* former British Prime Minister Tony Blair writes, "In order to instill discipline, into the party and even my close team, I was the eternal warrior against complacency."[8] In order to be an effective servant leader, one must be unwilling to operate in complacency—rather, the leader should be inspired and inspire change for the better.

For the servant leader, having faith is an important foundation for "living out" the trait of faithfulness.

Probably the person most closely associated with the word *faith* in the canon of the Hebrew Bible is Abraham. Though many of his actions show his faithfulness, it is most evident in Genesis 22, when he was willing to sacrifice his only son, Isaac, because he believed God's promise ("In Isaac shall your seed be called"), and believed that God was capable of raising Isaac from the dead in order to fulfill it.

Here's the way this story goes down.

God spoke to Abraham and told him to take his son, Isaac, to a faraway mountain and sacrifice him as a burnt offering. (Yes, we realize that some Bible stories can be quite graphic. But please don't let this cause you to miss the underlying point.)

So Abraham got up early the next day, packed wood to build a fire, and set off with two of his servants and young Isaac. When they had traveled about two days, Abraham left the servants behind and went up the mountain with his son. During the climb, it occurred to Isaac that they had plenty of firewood but no lamb to sacrifice, so he asked his father why.

Abraham replied, "God himself will provide the lamb for the burnt offering, my son." When they reached their destination on the third day, Abraham built the altar, laid the wood on it, and then bound Isaac and laid him on the altar.

At the very moment he took his knife and was about to plunge it into his terrified son, the angel of God called out from heaven, "Abraham, stop!"

Abraham breathed a massive sigh of relief and put down his knife. The angel told him not to harm Isaac. God knew Abraham was willing to follow Him and obey Him, because he had not withheld his only son from Him.

At that moment, Abraham looked up and saw a ram caught in the brush, so he captured it and offered it up for a burnt offering— as a substitute for his own son, Isaac.

Hebrews 11:17–19 offers a summary of the story "By faith, Abraham, at the time of testing, offered Isaac back to God. Acting in faith, he was as ready to return the promised son, his only son, as he had been to receive him—and this after he had already been told, 'Your descendants shall come from Isaac.' Abraham figured that if God wanted to, he could raise the dead. In a sense, that's what happened when he received Isaac back, alive from off the altar."

Abraham had no advance notice that his son would not die that day as the result of a sharp blade through the heart. But he did have faith that God's promise would be fulfilled. Abraham was faithful because of his faith—he was able to visualize what he could not see.

Servant leaders who have faith have no reason not to be faithful. They believe in the future outcome!

REFLECTION QUESTIONS

1. Are you faithful to yourself? Have you contradicted your principles to go along with someone else and avoid "rocking the boat"? Think about the last time you stuck to your principles and refused to bend to the will of another. How did you feel?

2. Consider your team. If you are currently operating as a servant leader, think of that team. If not, consider those you influence in your life (family, friends, etc.). How have you demonstrated your faithfulness to them in the past month?

3. What is your "cause"? Are you faithful to it? Do you work to ensure your cause reaches the desired outcome?

ACTION SUGGESTION

Focus on your faith. What do you believe in that you can't see? Can you visualize the end result of your faith? Abraham was willing to place Isaac on the altar because he had faith that God would not let his son be taken from him. What have you sacrificed for your faith lately? Practice an active faith; be deliberate about it.

CHAPTER SEVEN

ACCEPTANCE

—

"God grant me the serenity to accept the things I cannot change; courage to change the things I can; and wisdom to know the difference."

—REINHOLD NIEBUHR

THIS WILL BE A DIFFICULT CHAPTER for us to write. You see, we believe acceptance is one of the most challenging things we, as human beings, ever face. We're not just talking about servant leaders—we're talking about all of us.

We are faced with four forms of acceptance:

- We have to learn to accept ourselves, and that means both our gifts and our shortcomings.

- We have to learn to accept the outcomes, the natural consequences of our decisions.

- We have to learn to accept what other people in our lives bring to us, both the good and the bad.

- We have to accept the situations, the circumstances that come into our lives, because most of them actually become our training ground.

Usually we don't have any choice in these matters. They just happen.

Everyone who has a heart for servant leadership is going to go through some "basic training." It may be difficult—it may be unbelievably challenging—but it will be worth it. Because when we use the words "has a heart for servant leadership," we really mean the servant's heart will be softened to prepare him or her for the roles that are ahead.

William Shakespeare once penned, "Let me embrace thee, sour adversity, for wise men say it's the wisest course."[1] It's natural to want to avoid adversity; however, a servant leader understands that some of the greatest challenges can serve as the greatest learning opportunities.

"A leader embraces adversity as a forging tool in life. Most people do their utmost to avoid adversity. Some deny any benefit associated with adversity. A leader, in contrast, evaluates the situation, reconnects with his greater purpose in life, seeks to create options for handling the adversity and then takes action to create his future beyond the adversity."[2]

> "If you can't discover how to lead and serve the people closest to you—in your home and family—don't count on making much of an impact anywhere else.

For the two of us, our basic training was essentially home schooling. We didn't have to go beyond our own comfortable world to learn what it means to lead and serve at the same time.

Before we tell you our personal story, we want to make an important observation: If you can't discover how to lead and serve the people closest to you—in your home and family—don't count on making much of an impact anywhere else. Begin by serving your spouse, your children, your parents, or your siblings. If you have no spouse, no children, no parents or other family, or if they are removed by distance or their own distancing, there are friends and coworkers you can count as your family. Yes, the family of humankind is your family.

Our home schooling took place in what was essentially a single class—a single course. It was a course through which we learned the three basic principles of acceptance:

1. We learned to accept the situation that came into our lives—something that was unexpectedly thrust upon us. We learned to accept our circumstances.

2. We learned to accept whatever the outcome might be.

3. We learned to accept the role of others in our lives. We learned to let them do the things we couldn't do on our own. We welcomed the involvement of servant leaders in our lives. (And, honestly, we were stunned by their unexpected contributions.)

While we believe in these principles of acceptance, we want to add that we do not believe that acceptance means giving up or looking at your situation with a "whatever" attitude. We learned that acceptance can only take place following full engagement and active participation. Life is meant to be *lived*, not merely *observed*.

Here's our personal story.

On December 29, 1986, our third son (and this is a mouthful!), Graham Timothy Buntain Wilkerson, was born.

Just as his two older brothers had been from birth, he was the joy of our hearts. We brought him home from the hospital and all was well in our world.

Continuing the story from Rich's perspective . . .

. . .

Six months later, I was in Cocoa Beach, Florida, speaking at a conference on the beach. It was a great event, and I was having a wonderful time. While I was speaking, I got an urgent message from Robyn. So I went back to the room as quickly as possible and I called her.

"Rich, I have bad news," she began. Even over the phone, I could tell that she had been crying. "This afternoon I took Graham to the doctor because he has an ear infection and he's been on antibiotics. He just didn't seem to be getting better."

All of our boys battled ear infections as little kids and had been treated by the same doctor. The doctor said, "Just keep him on Amoxicillin and children's Tylenol, and he'll be fine."

When Robyn got home, she was met by her very concerned mother, who, with her dad, lived next door to us. Graham was in his car seat, so she put him on the kitchen table.

Mom looked at him and said, "Get this boy back in the car and take him immediately to Mary Bridge Children's Hospital! He's dying!"

Robyn responded, "Well, Mom I just got back from the doctor and he says—"

Mom repeated, *"Get him in the car, he's dying!"*

My mother-in-law is Norwegian and has always been very even-tempered—no highs, no lows, so the urgency in her voice convinced Robyn to rush Graham to the hospital. When she was nearly at the entrance, Graham had a grand mal seizure—now known as a tonic-clonic seizure. She witnessed his violent muscle contractions, and he lost consciousness, so she drove directly to the emergency room. She rushed in; they grabbed him and took him into a back room. All Robyn could hear was the staff screaming, "Code blue!" She didn't know what was going on, and they wouldn't let her accompany our son.

Thirty or forty minutes later, a doctor came out and said, "We lost him for ten minutes, but he's been revived and he seems stabilized. He's in a deep coma and it appears that he has spinal meningitis H-Flu bacterial infection. He has swelling in his brain. His temperature spiked at 107 degrees. We don't think he'll live through the night, Mrs. Wilkerson."

Robyn was in utter shock. She never imagined anything like this happening to any of her sons.

The doctor continued: "Here's the situation. Even if he does live, there's a very high probability that he'll be deaf and blind— and severely retarded. He will be in a vegetative state. He will lie in a crib and drool until the age of forty . . . if he somehow lives that long. You've told me that you are God-fearing people, so I'm sure you'll be praying. But if I were you, I would pray that the boy would die."

As my wife was telling me the story, we were both sobbing uncontrollably. "Can you get home?" she pleaded. "Can you come now? We need you. I need you. Graham needs you."

I couldn't believe what I was hearing. I promised her, "I'll get out of here somehow."

When I got off the phone, I checked with United Airlines. There were no more flights out of Orlando that night, but they said, "There is a Delta flight that we'll get you on. It leaves in an hour and a half."

It was about ten o'clock, and I was an hour from the airport. I had friends rush me to the airport and drop me at the curb. I walked onto the plane, they shut the door behind me, and I flew for most of the night. I arrived in Seattle early in the morning, and my father-in-law picked me up at the airport. He had obviously been crying, but driving through more tears, he somehow got me to the hospital.

. . .

Over the next six days, Graham's life was in the balance. He was in a deep coma the entire time. They finally had to do surgery. They inserted a feeding tube in his stomach and a shunt into his brain.

We were at the hospital day and night. We ate and slept there. Of course, when we were awake, we were praying for some kind of divine intervention. The doctors had made it clear that there was little—if anything—they could do.

We've always been people who believe. We never lost hope, because we couldn't accept that this child had been given to us so that we would one day pray that he would die. We've always believed in living . . . in life.

On the sixth day, we were standing on one side of his bed, a nurse was on the other side, and a hospital employee came into the room with our meals. Somehow, she stumbled and dropped the tray of plates. They crashed on the floor, and, at that instant, Graham jumped in his bed and began to scream.

The nurse started crying and exclaimed, "Oh, my God! He can hear."

That began the turnaround for Graham. About a day later, he opened his eyes.

The doctors quickly determined that he could see, because he would track all of their movements with his eyes. They said, "We don't know at what level he can see, but we know he can—and we know he can hear."

Just ten days later, against all presumed odds, we took our baby home. Graham is our miracle child!

For the next year, he lived on medications to help prevent any additional seizures. The doctors told us that if he could get through a year without seizures, they'd wean him off the drugs. That happened, and he's never had medications since that time.

Today, of our four sons, Graham might actually be in the best health. "Healthy as a horse," as they say—although our sons are all blessed with good health.

Graham is now in his twenties, but there were some difficult days during his recovery. For quite some time, the doctors thought hearing would be an issue for him, and he would have to learn sign language. So we enrolled him in sign language school. He seemed to hear everything we said, but he was having a hard time forming the words.

Even to this day, Graham has some speech issues. We, his family, all understand him, of course, and everyone who knows him well understands him. But if you were to meet him for the first time, some of the things he says are just a little difficult to understand.

Initially, he went to the same day-care center that his brothers had attended, and the teachers at the center worked with him as much as they could. Then we decided it would be best to enroll him in a special education school.

When he turned five years old, we took him to meet the bus at six o'clock in the morning because he had to travel from Tacoma up to Kent, Washington. Kent is approximately fifteen miles south of Seattle and thirty miles north of Tacoma. We'd often get tears in our eyes as we waved goodbye to our brain-damaged son in the early morning darkness—wondering how this would all turn out.

Naturally, we experienced some interesting times. From the ages of about five to eight, Graham was miserable in his clothes. He insisted that his belt be pulled as tight as possible. The doctors told us that he just didn't feel comfortable in his own skin, so he got a sense of reassurance from wearing an extremely snug belt. We actually thought he would be in pain as a result.

Things progressed well in special education, but we wanted him to have more of a mainstream experience, so we helped start a school for special needs kids that was part of the Life Christian Academy in Tacoma, Washington. It's called the L.I.F.E. Program—Learning Is For Everyone. The school is still operating and growing nearly twenty years later. It was through this program that Graham began to learn about reading, and his development progressed in many other areas.

Back to Rich's story. . .

• • •

Graham was twelve years old when we moved to Miami. For the last two years that we were living in Tacoma, I spent a lot of time on the road. Robyn is a rock who never cries. But she would call me at night and she would be crying as she updated me on her day.

On one particular call I remember, she said, "Rich, I was at the supermarket today and I had Graham with me. He threw a fit. He took out a row of ketchup bottles. Then he laid down on the floor, spun around, and started screaming. I finally got him to calm down, and I was able to get him to the car and take him home. People were looking at me like I was weird and strange and crazy."

Of course, because Graham looked so normal at the time, she was afraid people were thinking that she was a bad parent. She feared that someone would intervene and call Child Protective Services. She knew this boy could only live and thrive with us, and her greatest fear was that somehow he could be taken from us.

One conversation we had was especially thought-provoking . . . and disturbing. We were in the middle of dinner when she suddenly started sobbing.

"What's wrong," I asked.

She responded, "Rich, what will happen to Graham when we die?"

At the time, we were young middle-aged people and he was just a child. But she wasn't thinking about that moment; she was thinking about the years ahead. What will happen when we're gone? Who'll take care of him then? Her love for him as his mother was at the top of her mind and the bottom of her heart.

Those were really difficult times, and it became apparent to me that I was going to have to cut back on my speaking engagements, and probably get off the road altogether.

In many cases, acceptance leads to a whole new life. Our miracle boy was now forcing me to change the direction of my life. Every time we are in a forced situation, I believe it is an opportunity to move toward something better than what we are currently experiencing. All of that led us to the opportunity to move to Miami, Florida.

. . .

When Jesus faced His arrest at the hands of Roman soldiers, and He already knew the certain outcome—He would be put to death by being nailed to the cross—He had to accept His fate.

- He had to accept the situation that had come into His life. He had to accept His circumstances.
- He had to accept whatever the outcome might be. He knew He was a servant to the ultimate cause known to the world.
- He had to accept the role of others in His life—in this case, His Father in heaven.

On the other hand, He fully knew what He was facing. He knew about the ridicule, the disgrace, the humiliation, the nakedness, the inhumane torture, and the unspeakable pain He was about to endure.

If there was a possible "out," He was human enough to ask for it. Yet, He was also fully God enough to submit Himself as His Father's—and the world's—Servant.

Here is what it says in Matthew 26:39: "He fell on his face, praying, 'My Father, if there is any way, get me out of this. But please, not what I want. You, what do you want?'"

In that moment of prayer, Jesus clearly demonstrated the servant leader's trait of acceptance.

You can never anticipate the circumstances that may come into your life, but you can learn the power of acceptance. In his book *Leadershipology 101*, one of our dear friends, Keith Craft, writes, "The thing is never about the thing, but every thing is about EVERYTHING."[3] The point Keith so brilliantly illustrates in this play on words is that, rather than focusing on the immediate problem, we would be best served as to focus on how that problem can help to prepare us for the ultimate vision and purpose we have identified.

The principle of acceptance is essential for a servant leader to move forward in the face of adversity, knowing that challenges can position us for necessary growth, if we allow them to.

In his book *In a Pit With a Lion on a Snowy Day*, Mark Batterson discusses the importance of acceptance as a servant leader: "Opportunities often look like insurmountable obstacles. So, if we want to take advantage of these opportunities, we have to learn to see problems in a new way—God's way. Then our biggest problems may just start looking like our greatest opportunities."[4]

David Goetsch discusses the courage it takes for a leader to grab hold of these obstacles/opportunities: "They must have the

> **"**
>
> You can never anticipate the circumstances that may come into your life, but you can learn the power of acceptance.

courage to stand up for their beliefs even in the face of adversity. Courage is not a lack of fear. Rather, it is a willingness to do what is right in spite of fear."[5] Acceptance allows us to view trying situations as a seedbed for growth and development.

It may not be easy. We all face challenges in our lives. We had to accept the reality that raising Graham would not always be a smooth journey. What *was* easy was to love him, value him, and serve him. All of our children are our treasures, but there's something really special about Graham. If you ever meet him, you will know exactly what we mean.

REFLECTION QUESTIONS

1. Think of situations when you faced adversity in your life, personal and professional. How did you react? Did you fight back, rail about the injustice of it, or did you embrace the adversity, learn from it, and move on?

2. Facing adversity, "a forced situation," is a difficult process. How did your life change for the better after you dealt with the situation and learned from it? Did you move toward a better situation?

ACTION SUGGESTION

Jesus knew the adversity He was going to face: the ridicule, disgrace, humiliation, torture, and pain. He knew exactly how much He was going to suffer. He willingly embraced the horror of His situation because He believed in the end result. When we enter a trial, a period of adversity, we are able to deal with one issue at a time, strengthening ourselves for the next trial. Think of a period of adversity in your life, focusing on the individual steps you took to deal with the situation and how much stronger you were after each step. Do you think you could have taken those steps if you knew how many more steps you had to take? Next time you face adversity, envision the end result, and believe in the changes that will take place in you. Focus on how the situation will improve your role as a servant leader rather than dwelling on the injustice of the moment.

CHAPTER EIGHT

LOYALTY

—

"Loyalty means nothing unless it has at its heart the absolute principle of self-sacrifice."

—WOODROW T. WILSON
(28TH U.S. PRESIDENT)

SOME PEOPLE BELIEVE LOYALTY means blindly following someone into the thick of battle, and probably dying as a result. We believe loyalty can and will lead to good outcomes and, as we will demonstrate through two stories, can even save lives.

There's an amazing story in the Bible that you are probably familiar with. It's about a young shepherd boy named David, who was chosen to become the eventual king of Israel. On the road to power, he faced a few obstacles. One of them was that he had to confront a fierce giant of a man, Goliath, in battle, armed with nothing but a slingshot and five smooth stones. (But, as they say, "that's another story.")

The king at the time was a man named Saul, and he was not an especially nice guy. He was jealous, petty, and very shifty.

Because young David was successful in his battle with Goliath, he was invited to live in the royal household and, as a result, he became a close friend of Saul's son Jonathan. "Jonathan was deeply impressed with David—an immediate bond was forged between them. He became totally committed to David. From that point on he would be David's number-one advocate and friend."[1]

Saul knew he had come across a good thing in David, so he placed him in charge of all of his military operations. When David became amazingly successful at defending Israel against its enemies, his fame increased, and Saul's essentially decreased. After a successful battle, the women would sing and dance in the streets, praising David. (Yes, David was a good-looking guy with a six-pack, so that didn't hurt!)

Here's more of the story:

> In playful frolic the women sang, "Saul kills by the thousand, David by the ten thousand!" This made Saul angry—very angry. He took it as a personal insult. He said, "They credit David with 'ten thousands' and me with only 'thousands.' Before you know it they'll be giving him the kingdom!" From that moment on, Saul kept his eye on David.[2]

The next day, David was playing his harp for Saul—something he often did. Saul became increasingly aggravated and suddenly hurled a spear directly at David. Fortunately, David ducked, and the spear missed. But this wasn't the last time this would happen.

Now Saul feared David. . . . So, Saul got David out of
his sight by making him an officer in the army. David
was in combat frequently. Everything David did
turned out well. Yes, God was with him. As Saul saw
David becoming more successful, he himself grew more
fearful. He could see the handwriting on the wall. But
everyone else in Israel and Judah loved David. They
loved watching him in action.[3]

We mentioned earlier that Saul wasn't an especially nice
guy—he was jealous, petty, and very shifty.

Saul concluded that his life might be better without David
in it, so he summoned Jonathan and some other servants and
ordered them to kill David. Jonathan, who, as you recall, pledged
his friendship and loyalty to David, warned David to go away and
hide. Then he pleaded with his father to spare David, reminding
him of all the good things David had done on his behalf.

Saul agreed with his son, but it didn't take long for the king to
change his mind again. Remember, Saul wasn't an especially nice
guy. He was jealous, petty, and very shifty. He concocted several
evil schemes and attempted numerous times to murder David,
even by sending him into the fiercest battles in which "ordinary"
men would have died. But Jonathan's loyalty to David stood firm,
and David was able to cheat death. Jonathan even developed a
secret code—involving shooting arrows—to communicate to
David when it might be safe for him to return. Of course, no day
was really safe for David after that.

David had two opportunities to get even with Saul for his
treachery. He had two chances to take Saul's life by thrusting
a spear through his heart. The second time, Saul was asleep in

an encampment. David snuck into the camp and took Saul's spear without using it in revenge. His loyalty to the king and his friendship with Jonathan had spared Saul's life.

There are endless twists and turns in the compelling story of David, Jonathan, and Saul, the shifty king. Obviously, we focused on the servant leader's trait of loyalty. Eventually, Saul killed himself and David became king of Israel. (If you want to read an entertaining—and, yes, bloody—story filled with lessons for life, read 1 Samuel, chapters 16 to 31 in either the Tanakh or *The Message*.)

In Jonathan's case, even the anger of his father, King Saul, didn't destroy his loyalty toward David. In David's case, even the threat of death didn't compel him to kill Saul when he had the opportunity—because he remained loyal to his king. The story of David is ripe with individuals who demonstrated insurmountable loyalty and devotion to those they followed, another of whom was Abishai. One of our dear friends (who also happens to be our son Rich's father-in-law), Denny Duron, wrote a book highlighting the qualities and characteristics of this extraordinary man, *The Abishai Anointing*. In his book Denny discusses the quality of loyalty stating, "When we genuinely love our leadership as we love ourselves, we are there for them in the seasons of life when they are faint, when the load is heavy, and when they are challenged emotionally, spiritually, or physically."[4]

As servant leaders, we are called to remain faithful and loyal not only to those we lead, but also to those we follow, understanding that genuine care and concern for others is at the core of genuine leadership. R. L. Bramble is very specific on the topic of leaders and loyalty: "As a principle of leadership, loyalty must be viewed as a two-way street. If leaders are to expect loyalty from their followers, they must be loyal in return. There are three levels of loyalty that the Christian leader should practice: loyalty to God, loyalty to superiors, and loyalty to followers."[5]

We mentioned early in this chapter that loyalty can save lives. David's story is one example. But here's another story that is very personal to us.

In 1912, a young man named Gauthe Larson Hiim (later changed to Gust Hime), decided to head into the unknown to

> As servant leaders, we are called to remain faithful and loyal not only to those we lead, but also to those we follow, understanding that genuine care and concern for others is at the core of genuine leadership.

seek his fortune. Gust, the son of Lars Kjestheim and Barbro Moe (there *won't* be a test on this later!) was born in the small town of Sand, near Stavanger, Norway. When he was only twenty years old, he left the comfort of his home to build a new life for himself in the Promised Land—America!

To cross the Atlantic to get to America from Norway, Gust had to depart from England. He traveled on the old Stavangar Fjord boat, and when he got to England, he purchased tickets for two to travel by ship to America. His cousin, Lars, was still in Stavangar, but was planning to meet him at the dock on the date of their scheduled departure.

On the day the ship was scheduled to sail, Gust stood on the dock and waited and waited . . . and waited some more. He paced around, scanning everywhere for his cousin. As the ship was about to leave the port, Gust received word that Lars had gotten ill, and was unable to make the voyage.

Out of loyalty, Gust declared, "If my cousin and my friend can't join me, I'm not leaving. I won't go without him." So he sold the two tickets to someone at the dock before the ship sailed that day.

Gust's hope for a new life in a new land was temporarily dashed, but Lars recovered from his illness and the two of them were able to buy tickets for passage on another ship. The reason this story is personal to us is because it turns out that Gust was Robyn's grandfather. He served as a tremendous example of loyalty in action.

We've always had an interest in great ships, so in 2007, we took Robyn's parents, Fulton and Lorraine Buntain, to Victoria, British Columbia, from their home in Tacoma. We traveled by ferryboat, and it was a beautiful trip. One of the things we all wanted to see was an exhibit of relics taken from the wreckage of the Titanic, long submerged at the bottom of the Atlantic Ocean. Of course, we had seen James Cameron's Oscar-winning movie, so that only intensified our interest.

Upon entering the exhibit, we were each handed a replica of the boarding passes issued to passengers of the Titanic. Each pass bore the name of a person who had boarded the ship. Once we were inside the exhibit, we were able to check the name on our pass against the passenger manifest, to discover whether that individual was rescued or whether he or she perished. Sadly, when we checked the names on our tickets, we discovered that most of them had died in that terrible tragedy.

As we walked out of the exhibit, Robyn's mother said, "You know, my father was supposed to be on the Titanic. But his loyalty to his cousin, Lars, saved his life."

We were both stunned. We didn't know that—we had no idea. In fact, Lorraine told us that she and her sisters didn't even know the story themselves until after their father's funeral in 1965. When Grandma Hime related the story to her daughters, it was as if it were no big deal. "He didn't get on the boat, so he didn't die." There must be something unique about Norwegians: no highs, no lows . . . just a very even-keel way of approaching life.

Before the hit movie, no one thought that much about the Titanic disaster, so no one brought it up. But we can't imagine the ways in which our worlds would have been completely different had Gust Hime deserted his cousin and boarded the Titanic over 100 years ago.

Loyalty can change lives—and it can even save lives!

In looking back on the purest meanings of loyalty, we conclude three things:

Loyalty is not self-serving. It would likely have been easy for Grandpa Gust to decide, "I want to go to America now . . . so I'm leaving on the Titanic without Lars. See ya later, buddy." Gust gave up on his immediate dream in order to embark on the "great adventure" in the company of his cousin.

Loyalty is enduring. Once Jonathan decided to be loyal to his friend David, even threats of death did not dissuade him. The two young men were friends to the end. Unless you are utterly betrayed, changing times and changing circumstances should not impact your loyalty.

Loyalty is love in action. One of the most recognized statements of loyalty in today's society is defined by the historical marriage vows repeated at countless weddings: "to have and to hold, from this day forward, for better, for worse, for richer, for poorer, in sickness and in health, until death do us part." "Loyalty is not just a feeling that can't be perceived; it is a behavior or a series of behaviors. Loyalty is like love. The person who claims loyalty then does not exhibit loyal behavior is not loyal, just as the person who claims to love then does not behave accordingly, does not love."[6]

Your loyalty, as a servant leader, is one of the most remarkable and highly prized gifts you can give to those you love and serve. It's a trait that truly transforms ordinary people into extraordinary leaders!

REFLECTION QUESTIONS

1. As a servant leader, where do your loyalties lie? Are your team members loyal to you?

2. Has loyalty ever saved you from a difficult situation? Was it your loyalty to another person or another person's loyalty to you?

3. We conclude three things about loyalty: it's not self-serving, it's enduring, and it's love in action. What does loyalty mean to you?

ACTION SUGGESTION

Spend a bit of time thinking of loyalty as a gift, a highly prized and longed for gift. Who do you give this gift to? Who do you receive it from? Talk to those people, and let them know how precious you consider their loyalty to be.

CHAPTER NINE

HUMILITY

"If I have seen further than others, it is by standing upon the shoulders of giants."
—ISAAC NEWTON

THERE ARE THOSE—maybe even some of you who are reading these words right now—who somehow believe the only effective servant leaders are those who have power, or influence, or superhuman abilities, or unbelievable wealth.

After all, who are the people you read about or hear about in the news?

There's superstar Bono, lead singer of U2. He gives, and gives, and gives.

There's Bill Gates, multi-billionaire founder of Microsoft, who appears committed to ridding the world of poverty, hunger, AIDS, and other diseases.

There's Bernie Marcus, cofounder of The Home Depot, who gave a gift to Atlanta, the city that helped give him a start. He donated $250 million to build the Georgia Aquarium . . . and he's funded children's hospitals and dozens of other worthwhile causes.

There's Muhammad Yunus, author of the book *Banker to the Poor: Micro-Lending and the Battle Against World Poverty*, who has helped women and their families live better lives around the world through tiny loans that most of us in America would consider insignificant. But those loans change lives!

The reality is, you may not be Bono, or Bill, or Bernie, or Muhammad. But you need to know that your name, accomplishments, or money are not what's important.

> **The goal of servant leadership is not always and not necessarily to impact many. It could be nothing more—or less—than influencing one person.**

The goal of servant leadership is not always and not necessarily to impact many. It could be nothing more—or less—than influencing one person. Protecting one. Serving one. Saving one. Patrick Lencioni, a highly celebrated organizational leadership consultant and author, discusses the importance of a leader's willingness to make an impact regardless of the "perceived" importance in his article, "The Greatest Leader." Lencioni argues, "The truth is, our greatest leaders usually don't aspire to positions of great fame or public awareness. They choose instead to lead in places where they can make a tangible, meaningful difference in the lives of the people they are called to serve."[1]

Great servant leaders are willing to serve without the prospect of ever being recognized, it isn't acclaim that motivates them—rather, it's the desire to serve others. "Servant-leaders think of others—their colleagues, their coworkers, or their employees before thinking of themselves and their desires. It also means they resist the temptation to bring recognition to themselves by focusing attention on the fact that they are serving others."[2]

The "least among us" (and we include ourselves in this group) can always find someone who needs them. They can find simple but direct and immediate ways to serve. There may be others of you who are reading these words and saying to yourself, "I'm too old. I'm too young. No one would ever listen to what I have to say. Who would even care?"

The amazing thing about true servant leaders is they can be of any age, any background, have no experience or training, and still have a remarkable impact. They can be thought of as "the least" of all people.

There are great stories from biblical history of people—both young and old—who became amazing servant leaders. You probably know the story of Moses, especially if you were raised in the Jewish or Christian faiths. (Or maybe you just saw the classic movie, *The Ten Commandments*.)

If not, here are the basics: Moses was the Jewish patriarch who hiked up Mount Sinai to talk to God, picked up some heavy stone tablets bearing the Ten Commandments, and then hiked back down the mountain only to find his followers engaged in all sorts of bad stuff.

You've probably also heard the earlier parts of his story. Moses basically started his life very humbly—floating down the Nile River in Egypt in a makeshift boat. He began life as the "least of these." In fact, Moses was described as "a quietly humble man, more so than anyone living on Earth."[3]

His mother sent him down the river in a watertight basket to save him from a death decree issued by the Pharaoh. As good fortune (or God) would have it, this Hebrew baby who was supposed to be killed was rescued, adopted, and raised in the royal palace by none other than Pharaoh's daughter. He was eventually trained to serve as a general in the Egyptian army.

When God called Moses to serve as His general and lead the Israelites out of bondage and to the Promised Land, Moses thought he was far too ordinary. In fact, he argued with God about his perceived inadequacy. Here are some of his objections from chapter 4 of Exodus:

> *"They won't trust me. They won't listen to a word I say. They're going to say, 'God? Appear to him? Hardly!'"*

And: *"I don't talk well. I've never been good with words, neither before nor after you spoke to me. I stutter and stammer."*

Finally: *"... please! Send somebody else!"*

Thankfully, God was able to persuade Moses (He *does* have that uncanny ability!) that no one was better equipped to lead the future nation of Israel out of captivity.

But Moses made significant sacrifices to become a servant leader. In fact, he never personally made it to the land God promised His people.

Yet, he was the man who carried the stone tablets bearing the Ten Commandments—the foundation of law and justice for most of today's free world—from the mountaintop where he communicated with the living God, to the people who looked to him for leadership.

Clearly, the humble among us can become our greatest leaders . . . not *despite* their humility, but perhaps *because* of it. "Humility is the ingredient that keeps leaders approachable, that allows them to laugh at themselves, that keeps them from taking themselves too seriously, and that keeps them learning and growing."[4]

Our friend Nelson Ruiz is an example of a servant leader who exemplifies "the least of these" principle of servant leadership and has, as a result, become one of the most admired leaders in our church.

Nelson is twenty-three years old and a great servant leader, but early in his journey, he went through many troubled years. We first met him when he was seventeen. He had caring parents who admitted to us that they didn't "get him" at all. They didn't understand him or his motives.

> Clearly, the humble among us can become our greatest leaders . . . not despite their humility, but perhaps because of it.

Nelson faced a situation in junior high school that a lot of kids are facing today—he was bullied. That abuse hardened and embittered him. He went through some parts of the Last Chance Program in junior high. This was a program created for the most troubled kids—kids who seemed to have no hope.

At the age of seventeen, he left home and lived on the streets of Miami. Imagine a kid that age on his own! He needed money, so his major emphasis in life became robbing homes—with a loaded gun in hand and survival on his mind. In two separate incidents, he was caught by police and charged with possession of illegal weapons. (As the result of what some might consider to be a miracle, both of those charges have since been expunged from his records.)

In 2007, Nelson attended Rendevous—known as "Vous" (like "Voo")—the young adult ministry at our church led by our son. Vous is a gathering of high school and college-age people—some in school and many early in their careers. It's a special time and place designed to foster supportive friendships and encourage positive futures. It still amazes us both that nearly 1,100 Vous-ers attend every week. Who would have thought!

At his first meeting, Nelson sat in the back of the room by himself, slipped out early, and didn't return for at least a year. But he finally got to a place in his life where he was so miserable that he decided he needed *someone* or *something*, so he came back to Vous. That first night, he spotted some pretty girls—need we say more—so he decided he would join one of our servant leader teams, just so he could hang around with them.

At the time, we called the team he joined the Chair Stackers. We always have multiple things going on in our building every week, so we are constantly setting up, tearing down, and rearranging, depending on our anticipated crowd size. To accommodate our changing needs, we bought stacking chairs that are easily moved and rearranged.

Nelson got involved in that team so he could find a girlfriend and demonstrate that he was "all in." But he was serving for the wrong reasons—and he admitted that to us. Nelson was attending Miami Lakes Education Center, a high school designed for students who want to get into a technical job. Once they graduate, they have the benefit of a job placement program.

One day, Nelson was on the freeway heading to school when all his emotions caved in on him. (He would tell you that he had a "spiritual encounter.") He pulled over to the side of the road and began to weep as he asked himself, "Where is my life going? What's the point of my life?"

He decided to take a huge risk, so he told God, "I will give you everything I am, everything I hope to be, my whole life. I'm giving it all to you." As an apparent result of that decision, he came back that week to his servant leader position and took it over wholeheartedly. He didn't do this in an overpowering way or in a way that was demeaning to anyone else on the team. He simply couldn't do enough for others.

Everyone could see the change in Nelson—it was obvious that now he was serving for the right reasons. Even the girls he had set out to attract saw a change in him, and started to approach him. But he had a new interest—he was dedicated to servant leadership and to giving back what he felt he had taken all of his life.

He was committed to being a 24/7 contributor and became such a humble servant that, over time, he built a great team to help him. Ultimately, the leader of the Chair Stackers said, "I want to turn over this team to Nelson and I want to serve him."

Today, Nelson leads one of the biggest and happiest teams we've ever seen. They sing while they are serving, they have loud, joyful music playing in the background while they are placing the chairs—or stacking them up. He is an amazing guy in every way!

Recently, he changed the name of his team from Chair Stackers to Seating Engineers: Team Throne. Nelson told us they are setting up "thrones" every day for potential kings and queens. He believes God sees us all as kings and queens—as victorious people—so he wants the thrones set up properly.

You might think his approach is both unique and humorous, but Nelson is a young leader who understands and applies two of the essential ingredients of a true servant leader: availability and humility.

Patrick Lencioni captured the importance of a leader doing what may seem insignificant in his article "Stooping to Greatness." Lencioni explains,

> Though plenty of people in the world say they want to be successful, not that many are willing to humble themselves and do the simple things that might seem unsophisticated. Essentially, they come to define success by what people think of them, rather than by what they accomplish, which is ironic because they often end up losing the admiration of their employees and customers/fans.[5]

Servant leaders are committed to the goal of empowering and serving others, therefore they are willing to do whatever it takes to serve.

Don't ever minimize what you do to serve others! You may not always think that you're a significant "cog in the wheel," but you are. There is no servant leader—not even one—who is the least of these. Especially you!

It's not the proud and egotistical who change the world; it's those with the trait of humility. They are the ones who serve others without demanding attention. They are far less "ordinary" than they seem!

REFLECTION QUESTIONS

1. As a servant leader, do you feel called to change the lives of many or of just one at a time?

2. What role does humility play in your life? Do you struggle with the "temptation" of recognition?

3. Moses gave up a cushy life to become a servant leader to God's people. Have you made any sacrifices on your path to servant leadership? If so, how did they change your life?

ACTION SUGGESTION

Nelson takes great joy in doing what many might consider a menial task. Not only does he feel joy, he inspires his entire team as they set up "thrones." Our challenge to you: Take joy in the menial tasks God gives you, whether it be doing dishes, fetching coffee, or cleaning toilets. Enjoy your moment as one of the "least of these."

CHAPTER TEN

INTEGRITY

—

"Integrity is doing the right thing,
even if nobody is watching."
—H. JACKSON BROWN, JR.
(AUTHOR, *LIFE'S LITTLE INSTRUCTION BOOK*)

INTEGRITY IS AN AMAZINGLY simple concept—except for those folks who don't have any. And, sadly, our world is full of those people. To earn credibility and loyalty with those they serve, servant leaders must act in integrity. In his book, *Leadership Lessons of the White House Fellows,* Charles Garcia articulates this important fact: "By acting with honor and integrity, you build trust with your followers. The actions of great leaders are consistent with their words. Saying the right thing doesn't mean much. Doing the right thing means everything when you want people to follow you passionately."[1]

We believe there are three basic principles when it comes to integrity:

1. You *know* what you believe.
2. You *act* on what you believe.
3. You *teach* your beliefs to others.

Let's look at these principles one-by-one.

First, a person of integrity lives a life grounded in a set of beliefs unalterable by the winds of popular opinion or changing circumstances. Among those beliefs are, "My word means everything. I will tell you the truth in all cases. My promises to you mean everything. You can depend on me." According to our friend, Pastor Wilfredo De Jesús, in his book *Amazing Faith*, "A godly leader always takes the narrow road and inspires others to do the right thing. Leaders with a godly vision and unshakeable faith must exhibit humility and passionately pursue their mission."[2]

Next, a person of integrity will act on those beliefs. There are no empty promises. "I will do what I say. My word is as solid as a written and signed contract. I will not cheat you, even if I could get by with it. If I tell you I will give my all on your behalf, I will." As an example, if you say you love your child with all your heart, that's your belief. But if your child needs a kidney transplant and you are willing to donate your kidney, that's acting on your belief.

Third, a person of integrity will spread the "good news" of this way of life to others. In their book, *Lead Like Jesus,* Ken Blanchard and Phil Hodges discuss the importance of a servant leader not only modeling, but also sharing their values with those they serve. They write, "The spiritual health of the leader is the wellspring from which a follower's trust and commitment flows. If you seek to inspire and equip others to higher standards of performance and commitment, the best first step is modeling integrity in your own journey toward the same direction."[3]

As parents, we pass our values to our children. We may even have the opportunity to help transfer them to our grandchildren. Unfortunately, if there are cracks in our integrity, our children and grandchildren will pick up on that. Consistency is of primary importance. What we tell others we will do is what we must do.

Another, simple way of looking at this and remembering it is:

- Believe
- Declare
- Act
- Share

Once you have firmly established what you believe, you must declare those beliefs to your world. Then, you must act on the beliefs you have declared. Finally, you must share your beliefs and the underlying principles with the people you care for deeply. Barry Gibbons, in his book *This Indecision Is Final,* asserts, "Write and publish what you want, but the only missions, values, and ethics that count in your company are those that manifest themselves in the behavior of all the people, all the time."[4]

> **Consistency is of primary importance. What we tell others we will do is what we must do.**

Here's a wonderful story many of us first heard when we were children, known as "The Three Young Men with Amazing Integrity Who Were Tied Up and Thrown into a Fire Pit That

Was Hotter Than Arizona in July . . . Just Because They Had Amazing Integrity."

In the third chapter of the book of Daniel, King Nebuchadnezzar, the ruler of Babylon during the time when the smart young people of Israel had been brought into captivity, built a golden statue (we'll call it the golden idol) and set it up for everyone to admire. He made a decree that whenever music played, everyone had to bow down and worship the golden statue. Three of the young Hebrew men who had been captured refused to bow down before the golden idol. Because of their unwillingness, they were brought before the king. Their names were Shadrach, Meshach, and Abednego, and they were good buddies of the prophet Daniel, who was also exiled. (Those are some names, so we'll just call them the young men.)

Nebuchadnezzar decided to be a nice guy—just that one day— so he told the young men he would give them another chance to fall down to the ground and worship when the music played. If they refused, they would be thrown into a fiery furnace.

Somewhat loosely, here's the rest of the story:

The young men told King Nebuchadnezzar, "Your threat means nothing to us. If you throw us in the fire, the God we serve can rescue us from your roaring furnace and anything else you might cook up, O king. But even if he doesn't, it wouldn't make a bit of difference, O king. We still wouldn't serve your gods or worship the gold statue you set up."

Nebuchadnezzar, his face purple with anger, cut them off. He ordered the furnace fired up seven times hotter than usual. He ordered strong men from the army to tie them, hands and feet, and throw them into the roaring furnace. The young men, bound hand and foot, fully dressed from head to toe, were pitched into the roaring fire.

Because the king was in such a hurry, and the furnace was so hot, flames from the furnace killed the men who carried the three young men to it, while the fire raged around them.

Suddenly King Nebuchadnezzar jumped up in alarm and said, "Didn't we throw three men, bound hand and foot, into the fire?"

"That's right, O king," they said.

"But look!" he said. "I see four men, walking around freely in the fire, completely unharmed! And the fourth man looks like a son of the gods!"

Nebuchadnezzar went to the door of the roaring furnace and called in, "Shadrach, Meshach, and Abednego, servants of the High God, come out here!"

The young men walked out of the fire.

All the important people, the government leaders and king's counselors, gathered around to examine them and discovered the fire hadn't so much as touched the three young men—not a hair singed, not a scorch mark on their clothes, not even the smell of fire on them!

Nebuchadnezzar said, "Blessed be the God of Shadrach, Meshach, and Abednego! He sent his angel and rescued his servants who trusted in him! They ignored the king's orders and laid their bodies on the line rather than serve or worship any god but their own.

"Therefore I issue this decree: Anyone anywhere, of any race, color, or creed, who says anything against the God of Shadrach, Meshach, and Abednego will be ripped to pieces, limb from limb, and their houses torn down. There has never been a god who can pull off a rescue like this."

Then the king promoted Shadrach, Meshach, and Abednego in the province of Babylon.

These young men weren't afraid of disobeying King Nebuchadnezzar's command, because they only cared about doing what was *right*. "Practicing integrity means that your behavior matches your beliefs."[5] Servant leaders will be uncompromising in their behavior because their integrity arises from their unrelenting belief system.

Because of the integrity of Shadrach, Meshach, and Abednego, God delivered them from death (and perhaps even blessed them with a personal visit from his Son during their time in the fire), the king promoted them, and their enemies gained a respect and fear of God.

"Okay," you may say, "that's an interesting story. I'm not sure I buy it, but it was a fascinating illustration of the power of integrity. But what about today? How does that kind of integrity play out in the twenty-first century?"

Immacula Exumé is a native of Haiti. We've always known her as "Mackie." She is now in her seventies, and her life is wonderful, but many of those years were times of great challenges and deep heartaches.

Mackie was born in December 1939, the last of her mother's children. Her mom died when Mackie was two years old, so she was raised by her dad and two nannies. There were thirteen other children, in addition to Mackie.

Mackie was born blind, deaf, and mute, and it was the family doctor's opinion that she would not live long. The doctor was obviously wrong.

The family was Catholic, so as is the custom, Mackie took her first Holy Communion when she was seven years old. On that very day, she formed the first words she had ever uttered in her life. At first, she stuttered and was unable to pronounce her words correctly, but by the time she was eleven, she could see, hear, and speak. One day she simply woke up and could do it all.

Mackie was able to attend college in a country in which very few are educated, and she earned her teaching degree. She also studied English at night, and after graduation got a job teaching in a junior high school in Haiti. During this time, the leader of Haiti was the much-feared dictator, Papa Doc.

As a teacher, Mackie had a caring heart for all of her students. She wanted to equip them with the tools they needed to succeed in life. One particular boy refused to do his homework, so Mackie told him if he continued to refuse, she would have to meet with his parents. The next day, he again failed to bring in his homework.

On the third day, she was having lunch indoors with two other teachers when a student ran into the room and screamed, "There are many, many trucks and officers outside." Mackie looked out the window and counted at least fifty trucks and seventy-five members of the Tonton Macoutes—the secret security force established by Papa Doc to maintain his grip on power.

The school principal came into the room and told Mackie that the Tonton Macoutes had come to see her. The principal and other teachers immediately went and hid. Mackie walked outside, where she was instantly surrounded by dozens of men, all aiming their AK-47 assault rifles at her.

A man named Mr. Lassegue, the head of the security force, strode up to her, blew cigar smoke in her face, and spit on her.

"Who do you think you are?" he demanded. "You have no right to tell my son what to do."

It all came together in her mind in that instant. This threatening man's son was one of her students. "My job is to teach him. To help him learn."

"Well, now your job is to die," he scoffed. "You'd better be saying your prayers!"

The guns surrounding her all clicked, as bullets entered the chambers.

Suddenly, one of the young officers who happened to be dating Mackie's sister, ran up to Lassegue and said, "Please stop." They talked for a few minutes, and finally Lassegue ordered his men to lower their guns. "You are a very lucky woman," he said. "We were ready to execute you."

Mackie demonstrates the principles of this chapter.

- She believed children need a good education to succeed in life, and she believed all students should be treated fairly and equally, and that they should all be expected to complete their homework assignments.

- She declared those beliefs to the disobedient student, and also to those who came to kill her.

- She acted on those beliefs—boldly, firmly, and without backing down.

- Eventually, Mackie was able to share her beliefs with her children, all of whom are now successful adults.

There's often great risk associated with integrity. For the three young men of Israel, it involved being thrown into a raging fire. For Mackie, it nearly involved gunfire.

There is also often great reward associated with integrity. The three young men of Israel became leaders under Nebuchadnezzar and were largely responsible for introducing the one true God to that nation. Mackie has spent all of her life since those dark days helping others, serving others, and making a huge difference in countless ways.

In *Renovation of the Heart,* Dallas Willard defines character, which we believe is synonymous with integrity, like this:

> Our character is that internal, overall structure of the self that is revealed by our long-run patterns of behavior and from which our actions more or less automatically arise. It is character that explains why we use credit reports and resumes and letters of reference to make decisions about people. They do not just tell what someone did, but they reveal what kind of thoughts, feelings, and tendencies of will that person habitually acts from, and therefore how he or she will act in the future.[6]

A servant leader's integrity and character are the traits by which all whom you lead will measure you. It is imperative that the servant leader operate with integrity, because it is a trait of servant leadership that will never let you down.

REFLECTION QUESTIONS

1. Can you think of a time when a leader showed a lack of integrity? How did that make you feel? Does that leader's failure change the way you approach servant leadership?

2. The young men of Israel faced an impossible situation. If they bowed to King Nebuchadnezzar's god they gave up their integrity. If they didn't, they were to be put to death. This is an extreme situation for most of us, but servant leaders do face seemingly lose-lose situations. Can you think of a situation you faced that had no potential positive outcomes? Looking back, did anything positive come out of that situation?

ACTION SUGGESTION

Write down a list of the character traits you want your followers to measure you by. Look at them honestly, and rank them by those that are strongest in your life to those that are weakest. Pick a trait from the bottom of the list and make a conscious decision to improve that trait. Over time, work your way up the list!

CHAPTER ELEVEN

COMPASSION

"Compassion is sometimes the fatal capacity for feeling what it is like to live inside somebody else's skin. It is the knowledge that there can never really be any peace and joy for me until there is peace and joy finally for you, too."
—FREDERICK BUECHNER (WRITER, THEOLOGIAN, 1926–)

TO MORE CLEARLY EXPLAIN God's grand plan for life, Jesus often spoke in parables to the crowds that followed Him. Parables are basically earthly stories with heavenly meanings.

Chapter ten of Luke tells the well-known story of the good Samaritan. Jesus was speaking with a group of leaders of the time. One young lawyer asked Jesus what he could do to earn eternal life.

Jesus asked him what the Scriptures said and the lawyer responded, "That you love the Lord your God with all your passion and prayer and muscle and intelligence—and that you love your neighbor as well as you do yourself" (Luke 10:27).

Jesus agreed that this was true, but then the young man asked who his neighbor was. Jesus answered his question with a parable.

"There was once a man traveling from Jerusalem to Jericho. On the way he was attacked by robbers. They took his clothes, beat him up, and went off leaving him half-dead. Luckily, a priest was on his way down the same road, but when he saw him he angled across to the other side. Then a Levite religious man showed up; he also avoided the injured man.

"A Samaritan traveling the road came on him. When he saw the man's condition, his heart went out to him. He gave him first aid, disinfecting and bandaging his wounds. Then he lifted him onto his donkey, led him to an inn, and made him comfortable. In the morning he took out two silver coins and gave them to the innkeeper, saying, 'Take good care of him. If it costs any more, put it on my bill—I'll pay you on my way back.'"[1]

Jesus was illustrating that true compassion should not be reserved only for our close family and loved ones, but for all who need our care. The priest and the Levite passed by because they lacked compassion for the wounded traveler.

The Samaritan, on the other hand, treated the unfortunate man as a neighbor, bound up his wounds, brought him to a safe place, and paid for his care. The real kicker is that Samaritans were the object of scorn and discrimination in that era. Of all people, *he* certainly didn't have to help the fallen traveler. But he had compassion.

"Another interesting old story," you may be saying. "But do you have any recent illustrations?"

Yes, we do. Compassion in our day can take many forms.

It can be shown by the young mother in Phoenix who donated her kidney to save the life of a young boy she had never met. Because it was an anonymous organ donation, she never really expected to hear from the boy's family—and to this day, she hasn't. But she did receive word that he is still alive.

> **Genuine compassion for the needs of others prompts a servant leader to love the unlovable, to help the broken, and to reach the unreachable.**

It can be demonstrated by a community banding together to financially support the young family of a fallen police officer by holding car washes and street carnivals.

It can take the form of a group of friends volunteering to drive a man who underwent surgery for brain cancer to his seemingly endless chemotherapy and radiation treatments.

Compassion is a necessary motivator for the servant leader to serve. Genuine compassion for the needs of others prompts a servant leader to love the unlovable, to help the broken, and to reach the unreachable. While he was the pastor of the Healing Place Church, Dino Rizzo and his successor Pastor Mike Haman started a revolution of sorts entitled *Servolution*, in which they committed themselves as a church to meet the growing needs in their community. In his book *Servolution,* Dino shares their motivation as a church of servant leaders:

Jesus lived His life seeking opportunities to turn His love for people into action—everything a servolution is about. For us it's seeing our world, our communities, our work environments, and our families through the compassionate eyes of Jesus. It's allowing Him to show us where people really are, what struggles they are going through, and to motivate us to activity. It's taking the time to stop our busyness long enough to notice the needs Jesus is longing for us to meet.[2]

A fundamental quality of a servant leader is the ability to empathize with those they serve, to understand the struggles and needs of others, and a willingness to act upon that compassion. Walter Earl Fluker, author of *Ethical Leadership: The Quest for Character, Civility and Community,* states "empathy begins with openness . . . it assumes vulnerability and risk in the face of the other because as you see her face, she can also see yours."[3] He goes on to explain that empathy also opens the door for courage, because when we show another person empathy, we are recognizing ourselves in them.[4]

Sometimes the trait of compassion is a difficult one to learn and apply, as this story from our personal experience illustrates.

David McDermott is the director of operations in our ministry. He didn't arrive at our doorstep by accident. He's the same age as our oldest son, Jonfulton, and they grew up together. As infants, they were in side-by-side cribs in the same nursery. They were in the same preschool, had the same babysitters, and eventually ended up in the same classes in school. In junior high, they played basketball, baseball, and football together.

The boys went to a newer school that added a new grade every year, as the students got older. By the time they got to ninth grade, there still were no tenth, eleventh, or twelfth grades, so the ninth graders formed the varsity basketball team, as well as teams in every other sport.

That year, they lost every single game they played. They didn't have one win in any sport.

The next year, when they were tenth graders, both David and Jonfulton developed as basketball players. When the state tournament rolled around, their team won the first two rounds—all sophomores playing against seniors, in front of 7,000 people at the Tacoma Dome. Both boys excelled in their positions.

Naturally, there was great hope for the team the following year—when they would all be juniors. But one night, David disappeared. There was no trace of him and his family.

We found out later he was living in Longview, about ninety-five miles south of Tacoma, with his grandparents. His parents had gone through a divorce, so they decided the best thing would be for him to stay with them. Jonfulton, being a true friend, stayed in contact with David. Then, just before Jonfulton's senior year, we moved to Miami.

Fast forward five years. Jonfulton was just about to finish college in Nashville. David had established an extremely successful real estate career in Seattle. Despite the miles between them, they remained in touch through phone and email.

After Jonfulton graduated with a degree in business, he moved back to Miami to join our team at Trinity. Our business plan for the church involved buying a large vacant commercial building, using the 75,000 square-foot first floor for our ministry, and then leasing out the 50,000 square-foot second floor to ease our financial burden. (We believe that one of the things servant leaders are expected to do is manage their finances as wisely as possible. Doing so opens up even more avenues of service.)

When Jonfulton told David what he was doing, David said, "I can help with that!" Before long, David relocated to Miami and he and Jonfulton leased an apartment together. Jonfulton transitioned into the music department, and David took over Jonfulton's administrative responsibilities.

This turned out to be a great decision. There wasn't anything David wouldn't do. Work was one of his real loves. When he came to us, he offered to work without pay, because servant leadership was imbedded in his heart. He was at the church almost all the time. Some might even describe him as a workaholic.

David also turned out to be another kind of "holic." Alcohol took over his life. He was what is known as a "functioning alcoholic." He could still do his work capably, even though he was often drunk on the job.

Jonfulton tried his best to keep what he knew to himself—and counsel his friend as effectively as he could. Inevitably, though, word got back to us and we were both devastated. We decided to have an intervention and determined that we would have to fire David.

But when the moment came, we looked at each other, and our thoughts and feelings freely tumbled out. We don't recall which one of us said it first. But the words were something like this: "We're the church that claims we are here to help broken people . . . people in pain . . . people in need. If we don't help David—instead of judging him and firing him—we are living a lie." We decided, "Everyone else gets grace . . . everyone else experiences our compassion. David needs that right now."

When Jonfulton and David walked into our conference room, both of them were trembling. They were both certain of what would happen next.

David bowed his head. At that moment, we both "lost it." We told David exactly what he needed to do. He needed to enter a Twelve-Step program firmly based on biblical principles. He agreed.

Six months later, David was clean and sober. About that time he met a beautiful young lady named Carolina, three months later they were married, and they are now the proud parents of a little girl named Annalee.

Today, David is a key leader in our ministry. There are several morals to David's story, but the one that sticks with us is: "Never give up on anyone." In fact, we would venture to say that most people would be utterly surprised by the past failings of key leaders in our church, and yet isn't that servant leadership at its finest? Brian Jarret articulated how compassion manifests itself in the church in his book *Extravagant*: "The church is a combination hospital and command center, the place where hurting people receive comfort and the launching pad to conquer and transform the world!"[5] Being a church that welcomes everyone means we must be a church that demonstrates compassion, realizing that we all have our shortcomings and issues. But our inherent strengths as servant leaders make us valuable to one another, and of tremendous worth to our Creator.

REFLECTION QUESTIONS

1. The Samaritan in Jesus' parable would have been considered a person from the dregs of society, yet he went out of his way to help someone the pillars of society had ignored. This is the equivalent of a gang member helping someone a clergy member walked right by. Have you ever hesitated to help someone only to see someone in just as much need step into the gap? How does this story change your perspectives on compassion?

2. Think about the difference between sympathy and empathy. Look up formal definitions for both words. Why is the ability to empathize with others so important for a servant leader?

3. The story of David's battle with and recovery from alcoholism shows the value of grace and compassion. Have you encountered a situation where someone you know was "in the wrong"? How did you react? Would you react differently now?

ACTION SUGGESTION

Be compassionate! Take time to show compassion for one person you would normally walk past.

CHAPTER TWELVE

ENCOURAGEMENT

"You need to be aware of what others are doing, applaud their efforts, acknowledge their successes, and encourage them in their pursuits. When we all help one another, everybody wins."

—JIM STOVALL (BLIND WRITER AND ADVOCATE)

HAS THERE EVER BEEN ANYONE in your life who stood out as an especially positive influence? As a life-changer? As the one person you can point to and say something like, "He or she (the name goes here) is someone I will always remember because of the impact that person had on me."

We're going to refer to that person as your encourager. He or she is your "true believer."

Chances are that person exhibited a number of special traits. He or she:

- listened to you.

- viewed you as significant.

- affirmed you.

- cared about your "todays."

- hoped for your future.

- was generous with you—especially when it came to the gift of time.

A servant leader will not only serve as an encourager for those they lead, but will also acknowledge and appreciate those who have served as encouragers in their personal development. Encouragers help us to press forward when our backs are against the wall; they call us out of complacency and into realizing our potential. In essence, encouragers make us better.

"To encourage is to be a leader who, quietly and often unnoticed and unappreciated, makes a difference by manifesting a positive belief in others. . . . The value of encouragement is often taken for granted or missed completely because it tends to be private rather than public."[1]

In his book, *The 17 Indisputable Laws of Teamwork,* John Maxwell demonstrates the role of a leader as an encourager stating, "With good leadership, everything improves. Leaders are lifters. They push the thinking of their teammates beyond old boundaries of creativity. They elevate others' performance, making them better than they've ever been before. They improve their confidence in themselves and each other."[2]

We all have encouragers who come into our lives. "When we're on the brink of failure, the right words at the right time can keep us in the game. When we're too tired or discouraged to keep going, an act of compassion can give us new strength. There's no doubt about it: Encouragement enables us to persevere like nothing else."[3]

Many of these stories are very personal to us, sometimes because they are unexpected. But for us, for our family, and for the community we serve, our greatest example of a servant leader encourager is a humble man born in a dusty, smelly barn on the other side of the world.

> Encouragers help us to press forward when our backs are against the wall; they call us out of complacency and into realizing our potential.

We're guessing that no one who knew Him during His youth expected Him to amount to much of anything. He worked in His dad's carpentry shop, probably making tables and chairs and other simple but useful items. His family was not wealthy, but they supported and nurtured their son with everything they had.

No one really knows very much about his life until he reached nearly the age of thirty. Then, all of a sudden, this "nobody" burst on the scene like no one in history before! His energy was remarkable, His teachings were profound, and His love was boundless. His words of encouragement would draw and inspire huge crowds . . . and lift the spirits of individuals.

Here are some of his encouraging thoughts as recorded in *The Message.*

He encouraged freedom:

"Are you tired? Worn out? Burned out on religion? Come to me. Get away with me and you'll recover your

life. I'll show you how to take a real rest. Walk with me and work with me—watch how I do it. Learn the unforced rhythms of grace. I won't lay anything heavy or ill-fitting on you. Keep company with me and you'll learn to live freely and lightly." (Matthew 11:28–30)

He encouraged a life of humble service:

"Do you want to stand out? Then step down. Be a servant. If you puff yourself up, you'll get the wind knocked out of you. But if you're content to simply be yourself, your life will count for plenty." (Matthew 23:11–12)

Not only did He encourage servant leadership, but He encouraged servant followership—meaning we shouldn't always pursue the typical rewards of life. We should hope to follow the best leaders—those with honest, pure, and noble intentions.

Then Jesus went to work on his disciples. "Anyone who intends to come with me has to let me lead. You're not in the driver's seat; I am. Don't run from suffering; embrace it. Follow me and I'll show you how. Self-help is no help at all. Self-sacrifice is the way, my way, to finding yourself, your true self. What kind of deal is it to get everything you want but lose yourself? What could you ever trade your soul for? (Matthew 16:24–26)

He encouraged faith in the unseen and the unknown. After all, as we've said, that's what faith really is.

*In Capernaum, there was a certain official from the
king's court whose son was sick. When he heard that
Jesus had come from Judea to Galilee, he went and
asked that he come down and heal his son, who was on
the brink of death. Jesus put him off: "Unless you people
are dazzled by a miracle, you refuse to believe."*

*But the court official wouldn't be put off. "Come
down! It's life or death for my son."*

Jesus simply replied, "Go home. Your son lives."

*The man believed the bare word Jesus spoke and
headed home. On his way back, his servants intercepted
him and announced, "Your son lives!"*

*He asked them what time he began to get better.
They said, "The fever broke yesterday afternoon at one
o'clock." The father knew that that was the very moment
Jesus had said, "Your son lives."*

*That clinched it. Not only he but his entire household
believed. (John 4:46–54)*

The key thing about Jesus was that He was an encourager
to all, even those who did things they probably knew they
shouldn't have done. No, He didn't approve of their behavior, but
He taught forgiveness to His critics and encouraged the people He
encountered to change their lives.

*Jesus went across to Mount Olives, but he was soon back
in the Temple again. Swarms of people came to him. He
sat down and taught them.*

*The religion scholars and Pharisees led in a woman
who had been caught in an act of adultery. They stood*

her in plain sight of everyone and said, "Teacher, this
woman was caught red-handed in the act of adultery.
Moses, in the Law, gives orders to stone such persons.
What do you say?" They were trying to trap him into
saying something incriminating so they could bring
charges against him.

Jesus bent down and wrote with his finger in the dirt.
They kept at him, badgering him. He straightened up
and said, "The sinless one among you, go first: Throw
the stone." Bending down again, he wrote some more in
the dirt.

Hearing that, they walked away, one after another,
beginning with the oldest. The woman was left alone.
Jesus stood up and spoke to her. "Woman, where are
they? Does no one condemn you?"

"No one, Master."

"Neither do I," said Jesus. "Go on your way. From
now on, don't sin." (John 8:1–11)

When He was breathing His last breath, He gave eternity-changing encouragement to a criminal who was being executed at the same place and time as He was.

One of the criminals hanging alongside cursed him:
"Some Messiah you are! Save yourself! Save us!"

But the other one made him shut up: "Have you no
fear of God? You're getting the same as him. We deserve
this, but not him—he did nothing to deserve this."

Then he said, "Jesus, remember me when you enter
your kingdom."

He said, "Don't worry, I will. Today you will join me in paradise." (Luke 23:39–43)

The Bible is filled with examples of how Jesus of Nazareth and so many other biblical heroes encouraged the people who looked to them for servant leadership. But, in many instances, our personal encouragers can be the everyday people we meet in the course of our lives.

Rich loves to tell the story of his encourager. In fact, Robyn has heard the story many times, and she still enjoys and appreciates it, "because of what this man meant to Rich."

Here is Rich's story:

. . .

Growing up, I was blessed to have a "true believer" in my life. His name was Talmadge Butler. I called him "Uncle Tal," even though he wasn't really my uncle.

Back in the mid-1950s, my family lived in the Bahamas. My parents were servant leaders who were dedicated to meeting the educational, medical, and spiritual needs of the people they believed they were "born to serve." That's how we first met "Uncle Tal."

Talmadge Butler was a lean, tall, muscular Texan. He was from Kilgore, Texas. He had that Texas "twang" when he talked, but he could sing like nobody's business. I think he could have been on one of today's talent competition television shows, had they existed back then.

Talmadge was a pilot who flew a supply plane from the U.S. to the Bahamas. He would bring the mail and deliver medical supplies to those of us who were working on the outer islands. He was our link to the things we needed. He and my dad were about the same age and, over time, they became best friends. They were both athletic and they shared the fact that they were both devoted family men. Tal and his wife, Marge, had a little boy named Stephen who was just an infant when I was three years old.

Every Friday, Talmadge would land his floatplane in the waters off Nassau and tie up at a dock near our house. Then he'd spend the night in our home.

Back then, we didn't have a TV. We did have a radio, and Mom had a record player because she loved music, but the radio and record player couldn't compare with Uncle Tal's stories!

This guy was my hero! He was more than Uncle Tal—he was "Uncle Pal." He believed in me, listened to me, affirmed me, and viewed my young life as significant.

I didn't know about giving blood or donating organs at the time, but thinking back now, I would have given any body part I had for this man. He was my True Believer.

Tal would buzz our house in his airplane to let us know he was arriving, and Dad would take me in the truck down to the dock to meet him. Tal would get out of the plane, tie up at the dock, and immediately pick me up. "Richie, how are you doing boy? It's so good to see you!" Then he'd kiss me on the cheek and say, "You know I love you Richie." I'm a grown man, but those memories still bring a tear to my eye. I knew I had a friend who would never fail me.

We'd have dinner, and as we sat around the table, he would tell stories about the outer islands and the people he had met. I would simply sit there, spellbound, until my dad said, "Rich, do you know what time it is? It's time for you to go to bed, son."

Dad always meant what he said, so I would kiss them all good night at the table and head to my room. There were twin beds in my room, and I knew that Uncle Tal would sleep in that second bed. I was both excited and comforted by that thought.

But even though I would get in my bed, I wouldn't go to sleep. I'd make sure that the door was opened just a crack, and I'd get up, stand by the door and listen. That's when the real conversation started. Talmadge would begin to tell Mom and Dad about all the problems on the outer islands—the poverty, the hunger, the disease . . . people dying, children suffering, and no apparent solutions to any of it.

Then they would start praying. I didn't really understand prayer at the time because I was just a young boy. But I knew this was something serious. They were talking to God, and asking . . . no, pleading . . . with Him to help.

After what seemed like a couple of hours of this, they'd say goodnight. I knew I had to run back to my bed, pull my covers over my head, and pretend to be asleep, because Uncle Tal was on his way to my room.

Uncle Tal would come in, close the bedroom door, open the closet door, and flick on the light, and change into his pajamas. Then, with me pretending to be sleeping, he would kneel down by his bed, and start to pray. I learned about the geography of the world through his prayers. He would pray for every country of the world. It was as if he went on a trip around the world, and he would take me on that trip . . . without even knowing that he was.

Then, with all the people of the world securely in God's care—or so I thought—Uncle Tal would place his hand on my back and start talking about me. He would say, "God, I ask that you make little Richie into a great man. May he touch the lives of thousands of people, may his faith bring faith to other people's lives."

It was almost like a hot iron on my back. After he finished, he would fall asleep on his knees. My dad would be waiting for Talmadge to snore, then he'd come into my room—even if it was three in the morning—and wake his friend: "Buddy, you fell asleep. Come on, man, let's get you to bed." My dad would help Uncle Tal into his bed Friday night after Friday night.

Then, when I was still very young, we moved to Kenosha, Wisconsin, and, at about the same time, Uncle Tal moved to Africa to deliver medical supplies and food to poverty-stricken remote villages.

Kenosha was a different life for me. I was used to the beaches of the Bahamas, and now here I was, surrounded by snow. My dad somehow made it sound like cold and snow were going to be a lot more fun than beaches. Dad always had a way of making anything sound good. It didn't work.

Kenosha had one especially bright side to it, though! It was fifty miles north of Chicago, thirty-five miles south of Milwaukee, and further south of Green Bay. I became a sports lover—especially professional football! I was always torn between the Chicago Bears and the Green Bay Packers. I loved them both until they were playing each other, and then it was a toss-up. I loved Bart Starr and I loved Billy Wade, so I always faced an internal conflict.

Sadly for me, after we moved to Wisconsin, I never saw Uncle Tal except for those rare occasions when he would come to Kenosha to visit. When he came to town, he would tell his stories from Africa, and everyone he met loved him. When he was back in Africa flying his airplane, we gathered all the money we could and sent it to him, every single month. It's the one way we found to serve a true servant leader who was behind the controls of a small airplane, helping others.

Somehow, once a month, Dad would scrape up enough extra money to reach Uncle Tal in Africa by phone. Before his call, he would announce to us, "It costs a million dollars to call, but I don't care. I've got to call Tal."

The last call took place one bitterly cold Sunday.

Every Sunday night, a group of about fifteen or twenty people would go to a restaurant in Kenosha to meet and have dinner together. I would connect with four or five of my friends who were all the same age as I was. We'd sit at one table and enjoy hamburgers and root beer and conversations about quarterbacks, while our parents would hang out together at another table.

This night we were eating our meal, laughing and goofing off, and the manager of the restaurant came over to my dad and said, "There's a call for you in the entryway." (This was back in the days of coin-operated phones.)

Dad was out in the entryway for about fifteen minutes. I didn't know if that meant that he was on one call or had made other calls, but I was concerned. Because I was so connected to my dad, I knew something was going on.

I got up from the table to check it out. When I got to the entryway of the restaurant, the phone was simply hanging there. My dad hadn't put it back up, and his head was against the wall.

I had only seen my dad cry once before. This time, he was sobbing. I went over and put my arm around him and I asked, "What's happened, Dad? Is it one of my Grandmas? Is it Gran . . . which Grandma?"

I was sixteen. I was ready for any answer he could give me . . . except the one he actually gave me that day. He turned toward me and cried in my arms.

"Bad news, Son."

"What is it, Dad?"

"I just got word that Tal, and Marge, and Steve went down off the coast of Florida this afternoon. They're all dead."

Talmadge had been working to upgrade his instrument rating. He was with the number one, small-plane instrument flight instructor in South Florida. They never found the bodies, but they later discovered the wreckage in the Bermuda Triangle.

There was usually engaging conversation in the car on the way home from dinner, but that night, there was no discussion at all. Only total silence. Quiet. My dad's best friend was gone. They had spent their lives picking each other up. Now there was nobody to pick Daddy up.

I remember that night vividly. When we got home, we all went to our rooms and said nothing. I went to my little room, closed my door, and opened my closet door. Then I turned on the light like Uncle Tal used to do, and I took my clothes off like Uncle Tal used to do. I put my pajamas on like Uncle Tal used to do. I went over to my bed, I knelt on the floor, and I said, "God, I'll take his place."

Since that day, I have done my best to fulfill that promise to God and to Uncle Tal. I had an encourager in my life . . . a True Believer . . . . a servant leader who changed my life.

You can be that person for someone else. Do it!

. . .

We told you the story of our miracle son and his early challenges in life. But there is more to his story.

This time around, Robyn is going to tell the story of the encouragers who came into our lives because of Graham . . . and how, in turn, Graham became an encourager himself.

Robyn's story:

. . .

Our first Sunday after our move to Miami, Rich presented his thoughts to the church. He said, "I want to start a men's group, so we're going to start it tonight." (That's the way he rolls sometimes. He just feels something and goes with it.)

He continued, "We're going to call this group the Mighty Men's Group. And we're going to invite all the boys. If any of you have boys, they can come. If any of you boys don't have a dad from this congregation, you'll get a dad who's part of our team. That way, whenever you come to this place, there'll be a daddy here for you—a man who is kind to you and loves you—a positive male figure to help you."

There were about 250 people there that first day, and they all just stared at Rich, probably thinking to themselves. "What is *with* this guy?"

My boys looked at me with puzzled looks on their faces that seemed to say, "Dad's finally lost it!"

Just before the meeting that night, I asked Rich, "Okay, what are you going to do?" He replied, "I don't know what I'm going to do, but we're going to have men's night."

"Oh, great!" I thought.

At about 5:30, just before the planned 6:00 p.m. men's meeting, Rich was sitting in his office—a rundown, destroyed little shack of a room—and he was making notes on a few things he wanted to say to the men. At this point, neither of us knew if we'd have ten men or twenty men, or any at all, but he told me he knew he had to offer something significant to them.

As he was thinking and writing, the rickety door to his rickety office opened, and there was a little boy standing there. He appeared to be about the same age as Graham—about twelve years old—and he was African-American.

I'll never forget Rich's description. The boy was about as wide as he was tall—much like Graham—but, at the same time, strikingly handsome in his youth. He was "intensely black." Rich only added that because, at that time, Graham was "intensely white." Our boy's face was so white it would practically glow in the dark. It could take a while to get over the glare in your face—you'd almost have to look for some sort of light shield.

Rich looked up and said, "Hi. What's your name?"

He said his name was Elon. Elon Kelly.

He was wearing a pair of white shorts that went down to his knees, along with a red Tommy Hilfiger shirt, (because that was cool back then). He sported white and red-trimmed Jordan's hi-top basketball shoes, and he had splashed on some fragrant cologne that literally filled the room. Rich told me, "Elon was stylin'!'"

Rich asked, "Why are you here, Elon? What can I do for you?"

He hesitated for a moment, then finally responded. "You told us this morning that if we didn't have a dad from this church we could come tonight and we could get a dad from this church who would hang out with us."

"Yes, Elon, that's what I said."

"Well, that's what I need."

Rich looked in his sad eyes and promised him, "We can do that."

He then called Allen, a young man who came with us from Tacoma, into his office. Allen Griffin is also African American, and a tall, handsome youth pastor who was working with teens and pre-teens.

"Allen, this is Elon, and you're going to be his dad, because you're a part of this congregation and he needs a dad who's here."

He looked at Rich as if to ask, "What?"

Rich said, "Yep, you're his dad."

Allen said, "Okay."

Allen took Elon under his wing and they formed an amazing, enduring bond.

That first night of the Mighty Men's Group, there were about forty guys there, along with a bunch of boys. I watched from the back of the room. It was an amazing time!

The next morning, the church receptionist buzzed Rich's office phone. "We have a problem, Rich."

"What is it?"

"There's a man here who says he is the father of Elon Kelly. He said he has come this morning to kill Allen, because Allen has stolen his son. You better come out here because he's very upset."

"Oh man!" Rich told me later that this was a very frightening moment.

He went out to our little lobby, which was about four feet from our offices, and there stood a small Haitian man. With shoes on, he was maybe 5'6".

"Mr. Kelly, what's the problem?"

"Well, I'm all upset because my boy came home from this church last night and said that he had a new dad named Allen." He said, "I'll (blank) tell you right (blank) now, no (blank) is going to take away my son."

Rich responded, "Mr. Kelly, please, that's not what we said. We just said, 'If you're a boy in this congregation and you don't have a father in this congregation, when you come here, we'll connect you with an adult male. You'll have a good role model from this congregation to help you when you're here.' No one wants to take your son or hurt your son. We love your son and we love you."

He shot back, "But still, I want to see Allen."

Rich was obviously concerned. "We're not going to have any serious thing happen here, are we?"

"No, but I gotta talk to him." He was all worked up.

Rich called Allen on his cell phone and said, "Allen, get in here right now. Mr. Kelly's here."

"What?"

"Yeah, he wants to kill you."

"*What?* Is it going to be okay?"

"I think when you get here you'll know it's going to be okay."

Moments later, Allen, a big 6'2" hulk of a man who had traveled with Rich for four years on the road speaking in public high schools, walked in. He looked like Goliath peering down at little David as he said, "Hello, Mr. Kelly. I'm Allen."

Mr. Kelly looked up as if he were looking at a giant oak tree and said, "Allen, I just wanted to say how thankful I am that a man like you would come to my community and care for young men like my boy, Elon. I just came over here today to thank you."

In time, Elon's dad came to our church and became one of the ushers. In fact, he and his wife eventually became the head ushers in our church. They are remarkable servant leaders!

What I didn't know at that time was that our son Graham was going to be meeting his "brother" from another mother and father. Because that night at that men's group, Elon spotted my Graham and Graham spotted him. They became fast friends. They became inseparable. Graham was at the Kellys' house or Elon was at ours. Elon spent countless overnights at our house through the years, and his family became an integral part of everything we've tried to accomplish in Miami.

Two or three years later, we got in the habit of loading several of the kids into our two trucks on Sundays and heading out to lunch. One such day, Rich and I were in a huddle in the parking lot, deciding where we were going to take all the boys to lunch.

While we were talking, I could see that Elon was the last one getting into the truck with Graham, and all of a sudden, he stopped, turned around, and walked over to us. Unsolicited, he threw his arms around me, held me tight, then pulled back from me, looked into my eyes, and with a big smile on his face said, "Ms. Robyn, I love you. Ms. Robyn, a lot of people have been telling me there's something wrong with Graham. But I just want to say, Ms. Robyn, to me Graham is fine." He turned, ran, and jumped in the car. At that moment, I caved into Rich's arms, weeping.

When I finally got it together, I said, "You know what, Rich? I'm an idiot."

"What are you talking about?" he asked.

"I thought we had moved across this country to help these people. What I didn't know was that God couldn't move all these people to Tacoma to help us. The only way we could get help for our boy was to move here."

Without even knowing it, Elon had become my encourager. Rich's encourager. Graham's encourager.

For the next five years, Graham and Elon continued to be the best of friends. Elon went on a crazy, weight-loss exercise plan. He went from 225 pounds to 165 pounds and got accepted into one of the most prestigious dance and singing arts academies in the U.S.—not quite Julliard, but you get the idea.

He was training to be a dancer, but somewhere along the line, he just kind of "fell off a cliff" in his life. I won't go into more detail, but Elon lost his moorings—he lost his way.

We didn't see him anymore, but Graham never gave up on Elon. Graham would call us at the office from time to time and ask, "Mom, Dad, did you pray for Elon? Elon needs help, Mom. Elon's going through a tough time, Dad."

Graham never gave up on Elon and would call him and tell him, "It's going to be okay. You are going to be okay."

Jumping ahead in this story. . . just a few months ago, Elon came to see me. He admitted, "Miss Robyn, I lost my way, but Graham never gave up on me and I'm okay now."

Elon is back with us—just like old times.

Elon and Graham are prime examples of the power of encouragement. "If my goal is to encourage, and I'm committed to my goal, then my selfish attitude has no option but to be put on hold. That's one of the great byproducts of being an encourager: There's no time for wallowing in selfishness because there's always someone around who could use a shoulder to lean on."[4] Graham and Elon became each other's shoulder.

That's just one story of how Rich and I learned about "encouragers."

But there's another important truth here. Our needs change. Our roles change. Graham needed a friend—a servant leader—in his life. He needed someone to believe in him, unconditionally . . . and Elon came along and met that need.

Later on, Elon needed a servant leader in his life . . . someone who would care about him and encourage him unconditionally. And that was Graham. Elon became a miracle for our "miracle son." And Graham became the miracle that Elon needed.

Out of all this, Rich and I learned that every one of us—no matter who we are or what our circumstances may be—have special assignments to fulfill. We are all called to servant leadership. It's simply our role to respond.

REFLECTION QUESTIONS

1. Have you acknowledged and appreciated the encouragers in your life recently? Have you been acknowledged as an encourager?

2. Those who encourage us in childhood can have a vitally important role in our development. Do you remember an encourager from your childhood? How did they change your life?

3. Elon and Graham prove that a true friend and encourager will stick by you, even when others give up. Do you have a relationship where you are always each other's "best" encourager?

ACTION SUGGESTION

<u>Take time to</u> <u>encourage someone today</u>. You never know when the smallest compliment or kind word can turn someone's entire day around.

CHAPTER THIRTEEN

GENEROSITY

—

"The true meaning of life is to plant trees,
under whose shade you do not expect to sit."
—NELSON HENDERSON
(IRISH CANADIAN PIONEER)

GENEROSITY IS ONE OF the traits of a servant leader that doesn't come easily to any of us. Some may think that generosity is only for the wealthy because they are in a better financial position to give. Others may believe that the minimal amount they are able to give is too small to be significant.

Yet, we firmly believe that giving is one of the best gifts we can give ourselves. And yes, it is possible for someone who has very little to still make an impact. As Brent Kessel tells his readers, "The mysterious thing about the great reward we get from giving is that it's not something we can simply sit down and logically

> ## "
> Generosity isn't about what's in your wallet: it's about what's in your heart.

plan for. It happens best when our giving is as natural as possible, just a part of life, without 'shoulds' or 'musts.'"[1]

Generosity isn't about what's in your wallet: it's about what's in your heart. In his book, *Crazy Love,* Francis Chan makes an assertion that, we believe, captures the generous heart of a servant leader: "As we love more genuinely and deeply, giving becomes the obvious and natural response. Taking and keeping for ourselves becomes unattractive and imprudent."[2] The servant leader who genuinely loves the cause and the people they serve will not do so begrudgingly, rather they give sacrificially.

Long ago, Jesus made an amazing observation about this very thing, and He pointed out what He saw to His followers and to others in His hearing.

> *Just then he looked up and saw the rich people dropping offerings in the collection plate. Then he saw a poor widow put in two pennies. He said, "The plain truth is that this widow has given by far the largest offering today. All these others made offerings that they'll never miss; she gave extravagantly what she couldn't afford— she gave her all!" (Luke 21:2–4)*

You may think this story is irrelevant in today's demanding economic environment. How could someone possibly give his or her "all?" The fact is, we actually knew such a person. She was our Aunt Marie—or Auntie-Rie for short.

Aunt Marie was the oldest sister of Robyn's mother—Rich's mother-in-law—Lorraine Buntain. There were four sisters in all: Marie, Helga, Inge, and Lorraine. Marie lived her entire life as a single woman—she never even got close to getting married.

During World War II, Marie and her sisters served the military personnel at the USO Servicemen's Center in Tacoma. They would help with meals for those who were coming home on leave, or those headed back to their next assignment.

Marie also studied French and soon had a desire to go to Upper Volta in French West Africa (now Burkina Faso), to help others as a servant leader. In 1945, Marie traveled to New York by train and boarded a ship to Africa. It took roughly two months to get there, and she faced tumultuous seas and many discomforts in her journey.

With very limited resources, she almost immediately started a little school. She taught orphaned children, provided basic medical care and was, in reality, a mother to the fatherless and motherless. The people were drawn to her personality and her caring spirit, so they surrounded her with their support.

Marie was an extremely modest person who never seemed to ask much out of life. Her environment was utterly primitive— she lived in a simple hut until 1980, when she moved back to Tacoma. All those years, she never had running water, never had indoor plumbing, and never had electricity. In fact, during her last furlough in 1976, right before she went back for her last four-year tour of duty, her missions organization gave her an electric typewriter, thinking it would be a big help to her, but she turned it back in. She explained that it would be of no use to her because there was no electricity anywhere in her village.

During her thirty-five years of service in a faraway land, she never had more than $600 a month to live on. That was at the peak. And yet, she was able to start a medical center, build an orphanage (she raised more than 200 children as her own), open several schools including language schools, and develop programs to feed the hungry. She worked closely with local government agencies to secure whatever help they could offer.

Finally the time came for Marie to come home for the last time. At the time, Rich was traveling and speaking in public high schools across the nation. We moved to Tacoma from our home in Sacramento, California, to make our base of operations near Robyn's parents.

Six months after we moved back to Tacoma, the entire family piled into our big old van to pick up Aunt Marie at the airport. During the drive, we discussed all of our memories of Auntie-Rie. She always remembered our birthdays. Every year we would get cards in the mail from Africa—each with a $5 bill enclosed. We knew there were several months where she would only make $200 or $300, but she always remembered us. "That's love," we often thought.

We've all heard glorious stories of great heroes coming home from the battlefield to be welcomed by cheering crowds and marching bands. But when Auntie-Rie got off the plane, there were no crowds—there was no band.

Here was a woman who had given her life to the poor in Africa. She never married; she had no children of her own. She raised, fed, and educated orphans. She had invested her entire life as a servant leader.

As she walked toward us, we noticed that all she had was a brown paper sack in her hand. We all hugged and kissed, and then we said, "Let's go down to baggage claim and we'll get your bags."

"I don't have any bags," she replied.

"Oh," one of us said, "you must be shipping everything back from Africa in crates."

"Rich, Robyn, there are no crates coming. What would I have to ship? I don't have anything. The few trinkets I had I gave to the people in Burkina Faso. Everything I own is in this brown paper sack."

On the drive home, we were both really upset. We talked about it later. We were even mad at God, and we sarcastically thought, "God, that's incredible treatment that you gave Aunt-Rie. She gave her whole life to help poor people, and all she has to show for it is in a brown paper sack. No savings. No retirement plan. No nothing. That's amazing."

Sometime later, we both felt like we heard a voice say, "Marie owns what you cannot purchase with money." We suddenly felt humbled. We agreed that this is what the generous servant leader is all about.

Inspired by her generosity, we decided that we should do something to help this woman who had devoted her life to others. She had always been extremely generous. Now we wanted to be generous to her. Despite the fact that we didn't have a regular paycheck, we determined that we would give Aunt Marie $150 a month to help her out.

We gave the money anonymously, because we knew Marie well enough to realize that she would simply tear up the check if she knew it was from us. We continued to give her $150 every month until she died . . . some twenty years later.

We weren't the only ones who wanted to help Marie. Her sister, Lorraine, used her own money to rent a one-room efficiency apartment for Auntie-Rie. It was in a retirement center—a beautiful, six-story building with a full dining room and a great view of Mount Rainier.

Lorraine went to a thrift store and purchased a rollaway bed, linens and towels, some nice dresses, dishes and silverware, and basic cooking utensils.

Marie walked into that room and almost fell over in shock. "Oh my! I could never live here. This is far too nice!" Marie had lived in a simple hut for thirty-five years, so to her, this was like a mansion on Park Avenue.

Lorraine firmly replied, "Marie, this is where you're going to live. Get used to it!"

Having lived a life of service, Marie immediately found ways to be a servant leader in Tacoma. On Monday, she took care of distributing all the mail. On Tuesday, she taught English to Vietnamese immigrants. On Wednesday, she helped address mailers for a local charity. On Thursday, she fed people at the Salvation Army headquarters. Even though she was technically retired, Marie had a "full-time job" every day of the week somewhere. That's just the way she lived.

During that time our boys were born. She fell in love with all of them—but especially our oldest son, Jonfulton. When he got to be a toddler, she'd say, "Bring him over to my place after daycare. I'll take care of him for a couple of hours." She was very faithful in her commitment. They would walk together and talk together.

When Richie, our second-born, was older, she would include him so neither of them had to go to daycare or afterschool care. On Wednesdays, she'd often hop on a bus with the boys and take them on an "adventure." In fact, she eventually memorized all of the bus routes in Tacoma/Pierce County. She had traveled the world on busses, after all, so this was no great challenge.

Auntie-Rie and the boys would go to Woolworth's in downtown Tacoma. That's when there still was a Woolworth's, of course—also known as the Five and Dime. But the boys didn't quite understand the term, so they called it the Five and Dining Store. "Mom! Dad! We're going to the Five and Dining Store today," they would announce excitedly. "Oh, okay. Great!" we would respond.

The boys would always come home with some simple inexpensive toy that Auntie-Rie purchased for them. Of course, they already had plenty of toys—every time either of us came home from a trip, we would bring something to them that we thought was absolutely incredible. Yet, it was the dollar toys from Auntie-Rie that the boys cherished most.

Because of his travels, Rich was seldom home on a Wednesday. But when he was, he would head over to her apartment to pick up our sons.

Now, we both knew our boys loved us. There is an undeniable bond between parents and their kids. But when Rich would walk through Aunti-Rie's doorway, they would begin to scream and they'd run to hide. "No! No! Auntie-Rie! Don't let him get us! Don't let him take us! No!" They simply loved her so much! Rich learned that the best thing to do on those days was to go over and sit down and carry on a conversation with Marie, to let the boys get used to the fact that this was a change in their routine.

Here is Rich's story:

• • •

amazing story

One day, when I went to pick the boys up, I sat down to talk to Auntie-Rie, but she was preoccupied. She had one of those old business checkbooks—the kind with the big wide checks—and she was busily writing out checks.

"What are you doing, Auntie-Rie? Are you paying your bills?"

She started laughing as if what I had just said were the funniest thing she had ever heard.

Through her laughter, she replied, "Oh Rich, I don't have any bills. I don't own anything. I can't imagine having bills. That would be a miserable way to live."

"Oh man, yeah," I said, with thoughts of all my bills. "That would be just miserable, for sure. What are you doing, then?"

She looked up at me and said, "Well, Rich, this is the happiest day of the month for me."

"Why?" I asked.

She began, "I have to tell you a story."

"Okay."

"You know, all of my life in Africa, I was a taker. I wasn't a giver. I never gave anything. I didn't have a generous spirit."

"What do you mean, Rie?"

She continued, "I never really made more than $600 a month. If I had been a good speaker—if I hadn't been afraid to stand up in front of a crowd and tell them what I was doing—I probably could have raised more money and accomplished more. But I just couldn't do it. By the time I fed and clothed the children, I just didn't have an extra square dime to give anybody else. I just felt so bad about that."

I couldn't believe what I was hearing. To me, Marie seemed like the most generous person I had ever met! But there was more to her story.

"When I was flying home to America for the last time seven years ago, I thought, *I don't have any savings. I don't have any extra money at all. But if I did, I'd want to give it all away. For the first time in my life, I could be a giver.*

I had no idea where she was headed with this conversation.

"Rich, I'm going to tell you what happened. I hadn't been home for more than a few days when a check arrived here at the retirement center. I had no idea where it came from, because it was an anonymous gift."

"Uh, huh," I responded. All of this was suddenly beginning to dawn on me.

"I opened the envelope and found a check for $150 dollars. Can you believe that, Rich?"

"You have to be kidding me."

"No," she protested. "I saw that check for $150, and I thought I was going to die. The next month on the same day, I went to my mailbox, and there was another check for $150. Rich, do you know that for seven years that check has shown up there, every month, on the same day, for $150."

"I'm just shocked," I said.

"That's how I've been able to give to others. Rich, of all the hundreds of students that I raised as my own kids, ten of them decided to do what I did, and they serve the villagers. Now they have wives and kids, and they take care of the disenfranchised. For just $15 a month, those servants have some help . . . some help raising their families."

I was stunned, pure and simple.

"Every month, I sit down on this day—the day that check comes, and I write ten $15 checks to those students of mine. This day is the happiest day of my life."

Tears were welling up in my eyes. I did my best to hide that fact, but it wasn't easy.

I grabbed my sons and said, "Thanks, Aunti-Rie. Boys, let's get out of here." As I ran toward the elevator, I could barely see where I was going because I was crying so hard.

The boys asked me, "Daddy, what's wrong? What happened?"

I said, "Boys, remember this day. It's not every day—and probably never again in your lifetime—that you get to meet an angel. But you just met an angel today."

That's the power of generosity.

But what hit me like a ton of bricks that day is that it's important for every one of us to keep our commitments. Auntie-Rie couldn't have kept her commitment unless I had kept mine.

John Wesley once wrote, "Do all the good you can, by all the means you can, in all the ways you can, in all the places you can, at all the times you can, to all the people you can, as long as you ever can."[3] We believe the servant leader's generous spirit will motivate them to seek any opportunity to serve others in any way possible.

Not everybody who reads this chapter right now is going to be an Auntie-Rie—or a poor widow in Bible times—who gives it all. But we can all say, "Hey, I'm just going to be more generous. And I'm going to keep every commitment I make." That's just a better way to roll, isn't it?

Of course, after hearing this story, we gave Aunti-Rie an anonymous "raise." And, of course, she gave it all away.

• • •

As the nighttime infomercials on TV often suggest, "But, wait! There's more!"

Auntie-Rie had been retired in Tacoma for about eighteen years. She was eighty-two years old. She was comfortable and happy and healthy . . . and she was busy serving others every day of her life.

Yet, something deep inside her missed Africa. She missed her "children." She missed her team. She missed everything about Burkina Faso. When she received a letter inviting her to attend events that would commemorate the fiftieth anniversary of her work in Africa, she knew she wanted to be there, even though she knew there was no way she could afford the trip.

Her younger sister, Inge, encouraged her to make the trip. She even volunteered to accompany Marie, realizing that a woman in her eighties shouldn't be traveling that distance alone.

Then seemingly out of nowhere, Marie's years of generosity flowed back to her. The money poured in, and Marie was able to travel back to the place where she had invested so much of her life.

Little did she know that the 200 orphan children she had raised as her own had multiplied and had expanded her work beyond her imagination.

That day in Africa, the celebration of Auntie-Rie and her servant leader's heart was held in the local stadium, and 30,000 people raised their grateful voices to cheer her when she went to the podium.

This time it wasn't her fear of speaking or her lack of speaking abilities that had silenced her, it was amazement. She was speechless!

REFLECTION QUESTIONS

1. What does generosity mean to you as a servant leader?

2. People like Auntie-Rie are a rare breed. Can you think of someone who gives with such generosity? How have they impacted your life?

3. Take a moment to ponder John Wesley's quote. He advocates living a life of complete generosity, in every way possible. How can you implement this type of generosity in your life?

ACTION SUGGESTION

Focus on giving with your heart, not just with your wallet. What a difference true generosity makes, not just in your life but in the lives of all who view you as a role model.

CHAPTER FOURTEEN

RESPECT

—

"Every human being, of whatever origin, of whatever station, deserves respect. We must each respect others even as we respect ourselves."

—U. THANT (THIRD SECRETARY GENERAL OF THE U.N.)

THE U.S. DECLARATION of Independence says, "We hold these truths to be self-evident, that all men are created equal, that they are endowed by their Creator with certain unalienable rights, that among these are life, liberty and the pursuit of happiness."

If that doesn't mean we *all* deserve respect, what does? The thing is, the word *respect* can mean several things. And it can mean different things to different people.

But when it comes to servant leadership, we will use the words *respect* and *honor* interchangeably. When we refer to honor, what we're implying is that servant leaders respect, hold in high esteem, value, and prize one another.

Servant leaders who want to work together effectively—with great outcomes in mind—will observe these seven areas of respect and honor:

1. We will respect and honor our differences.

2. We will respect and honor our differing ideas.

3. We will respect and honor our unique positions . . . our special roles.

4. We will respect and honor our special contributions.

5. We will respect and honor our relationships.

6. We will respect and honor our commitments.

7. We will respect and honor our beliefs.

These are important things to discuss, because no two people are in complete alignment 100 percent of the time. If you are married, or in a long-term relationship, you know exactly what we mean. If you are part of a team, the alignment issues are easily multiplied by the number of people on the team.

Because of our inherent differences, mutual respect is an essential trait. We all come from different backgrounds— economically, ethnically, educationally, socially, spiritually, and more—but if we are part of a marriage or a team, we are likely to have many shared goals and values. "Respect takes on a whole new dimension when it includes respecting differences and coping with dissonance and diversity. Respect suddenly becomes more like a rigorous discipline, continually practiced and renewed, than simply a feel-good concept or lofty aspiration."[1]

Servant leaders don't view diversity in thoughts and opinions as a liability to a team's success; they view differences in opinions as an asset. In an article entitled, "Diversity's Missing Ingredient," Patrick Lencioni reinforces this notion: "The practical advantage of diversity boils down to this: a group of people with different perspectives usually makes better decisions and finds more creative solutions than those who have largely similar views, backgrounds and skill sets. This is true for all teams, whether they're running a corporation, a church, a school or a movie studio."[2] A servant leader will not only respect but will cultivate an environment in which diversity in opinions and approaches is welcomed.

Using the Susan G. Komen Race for the Cure as an example, everyone who runs likely shares the goal of curing and eradicating breast cancer. At Trinity Church, our servant leaders share the vision of helping others experience whole and wholesome lives. In both of these cases, the participants overlook their differences in order to work together toward worthy goals.

> Servant leaders don't view diversity in thoughts and opinions as a liability to a team's success; they view differences in opinions as an asset.

T. H. White captures this idea wonderfully when he writes: "I can imagine nothing more terrifying than an Eternity filled with men who were all the same. The only thing which has made life bearable . . . has been the diversity of creatures on the surface of the globe."[3]

The twelve people who first chose to follow Jesus were about as diverse as any group can get. They were fishermen, tax collectors, and political activists. Yet they came together to become "fishers of men," to proclaim the gospel of love, peace, and grace. Servant leaders make the deliberate choice to respect and honor their differences.

We also need to respect our differing ideas. Imagine how boring the world would be if every musician wrote and performed the same song, if every artist painted the same scene, if every author wrote the same book, or if every movie producer and director brought the same story to the screen. Author/teacher Stephen R. Covey wisely observes, "Strength lies in differences, not in similarities."[4]

Just as our backgrounds and ideas differ, so do our roles. Imagine again how dysfunctional the world would be if we were all bankers, or mechanics, or teachers, or cabinet-makers, or lawyers, or grocers, or airline pilots. The world would screech to a halt. That's why we must respect and honor our unique positions, our special roles.

Every servant leader has a special role to fill. Our assignment is to identify that role, and fulfill it. Faithfully, consistently, and enthusiastically! No one's contributions as a servant leader should ever be ignored, minimized, or disrespected in any way. It doesn't matter what you do. If you do it to the best of your ability, with an attitude of service, to make your world and the lives of others better, you have made a valuable contribution. Keep doing that!

Relationships are what build and sustain marriages, families, businesses, schools, churches, governments, and every other organization you can name. In contrast, dysfunctional relationships can undermine and destroy all of those things. In his book, *The Master Plan,* self-made entrepreneur Mike Ingram writes "Good things in life generally do not happen by accident. Successful partnerships are usually the result of attention and intention."[5] Servant leaders understand the importance of relationships and partnerships in their lives, and thus are intentional about cultivating and sustaining those relationships.

To sustain meaningful, successful relationships, it's vital that we respect and honor our commitments. A marital relationship is likely doomed to failure if one or both partners dishonor the commitments made during the marriage ceremony. Similarly, a business partnership is headed for a shipwreck if either of the partners fails to follow through on promises.

Of course, even teams comprised of servant leaders can fail miserably if every single member of the team doesn't honor their commitment. When we talk about respecting and honoring our beliefs, we are actually referring to two things: our own beliefs and the beliefs of others.

> **"**
> Every servant leader has a special role to fill. Our assignment is to identify that role, and fulfill it.

Here's the key: If you have a certain set of beliefs and another leader holds fast to beliefs that contradict yours, it's vital that you retain your own. That's not to say that there isn't reasonable room for compromise, but there's a huge difference between compromise and "selling out." If you abandon your vision or your values, you are abandoning the core of who you really are as a human being. Ruma Bose and Lou Faust III write of Mother Teresa on this subject:

Leaders need to know where to draw their lines. Sometimes you have to compromise. You need to have the courage to decide which compromises are acceptable and which are not. You will not always make the right choices, and you will get criticized for them. Mother Teresa was criticized about many of her choices. Her response was to stand by her beliefs and focus on getting her job done.[6]

At the same time, you demonstrate the quality of servanthood when you respect and honor the beliefs of others. Often, the ultimate solution to any need or situation involves blending the best ideas from all who are involved into a single best plan. In his book, *The Advantage,* Patrick Lencioni discusses the importance of healthy disagreement and differing opinions when working towards a common goal, "Two people who trust and care about one another and are engaged in something important should feel compelled to disagree, and sometimes passionately, when they see things differently."[7]

It is imperative that as servant leaders we don't shy away from discourse when working with others. Rather, we should respectfully accept differing opinions, understanding that the ultimate goal is serving others. One of the things we love the most about the people we serve at Trinity Church is that they respect and honor one another. They are willing to deny their own egos to support the cause—whatever it may be. They respect one another across all ages, backgrounds, and interests.

In fact, we've never heard anyone say anything remotely similar to "It's my way or the highway." Respect is the foundation of all the amazing things our servant leaders accomplish.

When we first arrived in Miami, in July of 1998, there was such a tremendous need that we didn't really know where to start. Like most people, we had our biases politically, as well as in most other ways. Here we were in our mid-forties, four sons in tow, with a lot of miles behind us. We were thrown into a completely new culture in Miami that didn't look or feel like anything we were familiar with.

So many of the people we began associating with were just flat poor. Basic comforts of life had escaped them for the most part. When people are thrown into a situation like that, several things happen. We quickly had to distinguish our values from our opinions. We had to decide what we absolutely could and couldn't embrace.

We found that many of our opinions didn't help anyone, and if we could set our opinions aside and press forward with our mission, perhaps good things would happen. And they did.

After spending everything we had in the first year, and facing what seemed like an impossible upcoming summer, one day Robyn spotted an RFP (Request for Proposal) posted in the Miami Herald. It was offered by the Children's Trust for summer day camps.

She immediately thought, "We need a summer day camp!"

We are situated in an area overflowing with little kids—and most of them are latchkey kids who live with a single mom. The summer day camp would operate for eight weeks, Monday to Friday, from 8:00 a.m. to 5:00 p.m.

Robyn went down to the county office and picked up the RFP, which looked to her as though it would end up being the length of a doctoral thesis. It took her about four weeks to fill it out. On top of that, she was competing against huge social service organizations in Dade County.

When she went to the meetings, she faced nearly 100 potential providers, and met with odd stares, as if to say, "Who are you? What are you doing here?" But we were in need. We had a bunch of children who needed a safe place to call home during the summer.

Robyn determined to be nice to the other competitors and treat them with respect and honor. At first they seemed to barely tolerate her, but it was difficult for them to repay evil for good, so Robyn began to receive pleasant responses from people because she offered respect first!

As if by some divine design, on her first attempt, Robyn was awarded a $175,000 County contract to take care of 250 children for eight weeks! The contract was written in Trinity Church's name, DBA Peacemakers Family Center.

Here we were, a church, receiving money from taxpayers to help disenfranchised children. We must tell you that never in a million years did we ever think our biggest partner in helping those in need in Miami would be a government entity!

Immediately, we asked pastor Linda Freeman, who has been with us almost from the beginning, to lead this part of our organization. She has developed a social service team that we believe is second to none in all of Dade County—if not the entire state of Florida.

Throughout the years, we have learned to demonstrate respect and honor when we meet with people in all government positions, whether we agree with their political views or not. Our value is children and broken people who need help. Because our servant leader DNA includes respect, we have received government support under Presidents Clinton, Bush, and Obama.

By the grace of God, President Bush publicly spoke of our Peacemakers Family Center here in Miami, and by the grace of God, Robyn and I have twice been invited by President Obama to the White House. Regardless of our political leanings, we have personally and corporately prayed for and honored all three of these Presidents, just as the Scriptures say, "Pray especially for rulers and their governments to rule well" (1 Timothy 2:2).

We believe our respect for a seeming impossible partnership has been the one servant leader trait that has helped us win $24 million in government funding over the past fifteen years—and as a result the lives of countless children, single parents, prisoners, and hungry families have been touched!

REFLECTION QUESTIONS

1. Working with other servant leaders can sometimes be difficult. How do you deal with a situation where the person you are talking to has drastically different opinions or values?

2. How do you appreciate the diversity in your life? Do you make a point of getting to know other people who are different from you?

3. Have you ever encountered a situation where your preconceived notions and opinions actually got in the way of being an effective servant leader? What did you do to rectify the situation?

ACTION SUGGESTION

Take time in the next few days to consciously think about how the people you interact with are different than you. Look at how those differences allow you to interact with each other. Do you make an effort to maintain solid relationships with these individuals?

CHAPTER FIFTEEN

MENTORING

—

*"Remember that mentor leadership is all about serving.
Jesus said, 'For even the Son of Man came not to be
served but to serve others and to give his life as a
ransom for many'" (Mark 10:45).*

—TONY DUNGY (NFL COACH AND FORMER PRO 1955–2008)

JUST AS YOU HAVE PROBABLY had an encourager at some point in your life, you might have also had a mentor. If so, you can likely recall with great appreciation the influence that individual had on your life.

The word *mentor* actually comes from a character in ancient Greek mythology. The meaning eventually evolved from a specific character to anyone who exhibits the traits of that character.

In the most basic terms, a mentor is someone who imparts both wisdom and knowledge to a less-experienced associate—wisdom being more timeless, knowledge being more current. This associate can be either younger or older than the mentor—age doesn't really matter, so long as the one being mentored is willing to receive the wisdom. According to John Daresh, "A mentor does not necessarily have to be an older person who is ready, willing, and able to provide all of the answers to those who are newcomers. Usually, mentors have a lot of experience and craft knowledge to share with others."[1]

In their book *Execution*, Larry Bossidy and Ram Charan stress the importance of leaders developing and mentoring those whom they lead, "Leaders need to commit as much as 40 percent of their time and emotional energy, in one form or another, to selecting, appraising, and developing people."[2] Servant leaders will not only welcome the wisdom and empowerment that comes from a trusted mentor, they will also be intentional about providing that same counsel and development to those whom they serve.

Breaking down what a mentor actually does, here is what we see as the essentials:

A mentor . . .

- teaches
- coaches
- engages
- praises
- corrects

That may seem like a heavy workload for anyone who has the desire to become a mentor. The reality, though, is that all these components are inter-related and they build on one another, so it's not as overwhelming as it seems. In fact, it really comes down to one word: a mentor cares.

Let's break it down by its individual components.

Mentors teach what they know. There's no pretending to know something—or faking knowledge. An effective mentor who doesn't know the answer to a question or a problem admits it, and finds someone else who does. Giving no information or delaying information is better than giving incorrect information.

Teaching provides the information the student needs to perform a task, complete a function, or serve in a specific capacity. In a recent article, "Love the Killer App," bestselling author and former Yahoo executive Tim Sanders writes, "The secret to being a high-impact leader and the essence of individual and corporate success: Learn as much as you can as quickly as you can and share your knowledge aggressively."[3] To draw a comparison with the game of baseball: Teaching imparts the rules of the game, the functions of each player, and the nuances of a play (such as when to attempt to steal second, and when not to try it).

Mentors coach on what they teach. It's one thing to present information to a student, but it's a significantly different thing to help that student perform, based on the information.

Using the baseball illustration again, the coaching aspect of mentoring involves helping the students execute what they have learned. It's one thing for a player to mentally know that the goal of the batter is to hit the ball and safely run the bases. It's another to actually execute a hit. Coaching bridges the gap between knowledge and performance.

> **It really comes down to one word: a mentor *cares*.**

Mentors engage the student in action. A mentor gets the student involved. It's not enough to know; we must all get in the game and do.

Back to baseball: A player who knows the principles of the game and has been coached to hit the ball and run the bases will never contribute to a victory unless he or she gets to play in an actual game. That's where learning becomes doing. Benjamin Franklin once advised: "Tell me and I forget, teach me and I may remember, involve me and I learn."

Mentors praise the student for achievement. This is the encouragement part of the mentoring process. Praise promotes greater effort and continuing improvement. "The mentor must be able to recognize the ability of the mentee and make it clear to the mentee that he or she believes in the mentee's capacity to progress."[4]

> "
> Praise promotes greater effort and continuing improvement.

Watch a baseball game in person or on TV. When a player gets a hit, scores a run, or makes a great defensive play, the manager and the other players on the team jump off the bench in the dugout, and the manager—the mentor—usually cheers the loudest. And when the team wins a game, or, better yet, the World Series, the victors rush onto the field to celebrate one another's big win.

Here is one significant piece of advice, though. Your praise must be genuine. The people you mentor can see through phony praise. They can spot it easily, and it diminishes your credibility as a mentor. So keep it real!

Mentors correct the student in order to build on knowledge and skills. Notice that we avoided the word *scolds.* Correction has nothing to do with scolding or punishment. Correction should be positive. "Try this instead of that. It might result in . . ."

That's why in baseball, there are batting coaches. That's why even champion golfers such as Phil Mickelson and Tiger Woods still have coaches who work with them to help correct small issues in their swings. Trust us, these coaches don't say things like "You incompetent dummy! You're such a failure!" No, they correct through encouragement.

> **"**
>
> Servant leaders welcome correction offered by a trusted mentor because they can be confident that the mentor has their best interest at heart.

A servant leader will be receptive to the correction offered not only by mentors, but by those whom they lead. In his book, *7 Lessons for Leading in Crisis,* bestselling author Bill George offers this insight "Instead of building an organization of truth tellers, many leaders surround themselves with sycophants who tell them only what they want to hear, rather than sharing the stark reality."[5]

Servant leaders welcome correction offered by a trusted mentor because they can be confident that the mentor has their best interest at heart. Furthermore, a servant leader should be willing to offer this correction in a loving and edifying manner, desiring to strengthen and empower those they serve.

But there's much more to mentoring than teaching, coaching, engaging, praising, and correcting the student. In baseball, of course, the goal is to build a winning team. But in the bigger picture of life, the purpose of mentoring is for leaders to replace themselves with others who are fully prepared—who are knowledgeable, skilled, competent, and able to continue what the leaders have started.

The greatest servant leaders pour their energy into teaching and preparing others to follow the path of servanthood. In their book, *The Servant Leader,* Ken Blanchard and Phil Hodges articulate the importance of a servant leader mentoring others: "As a servant leader the way you serve the vision is by developing people so that they can work on that vision when you're not around. The ultimate sign of an effective servant leader is what happens when you are not there."[6]

Servant leaders understand that their vision and cause are bigger than they can accomplish alone; they understand the importance of empowering others to expand their vision to a greater extent. Jesus did exactly that. He taught His disciples everything He knew. In John 14:12, He is quoted as saying, "The person who trusts me will not only do what I'm doing but even greater things, because I, on my way to the Father, am giving you the same work to do that I've been doing. You can count on it."

The reality is, it worked! A handful of loyal, trained followers brought His message to the world. The teachings of Jesus are now widely-accepted and followed by billions of people around the world.

The story of Moses and his student, Joshua, also illustrates the essential point that effective mentors do three things:

- They identify a suitable follower.

- They teach everything they know to that follower.

- They turn their work over to the follower—at the right time.

A great example of those three principles is found in The Tenackh, in the story of Moses. We've already told you a part of his story—the man God chose to lead the enslaved people out of Egypt to the Promised Land. And he was the man God chose to receive the Ten Commandments at the summit of Mount Sinai.

But Moses also provides a wonderful illustration of the principles of mentoring. The relationship between Moses and Joshua is a fascinating one. Moses was a great leader and was a great example to the young emerging leader, Joshua.

Joshua was Moses's right-hand man and a great warrior. But Joshua didn't become a leader by accident. The man Joshua became was directly related to the man who mentored him. It's a powerful example about mentoring "in the trenches." To understand the story better, let's look at the background of Moses—a story we've already told in part.

Moses was born during a time in Egypt when the number of Israelites was increasing daily. A new Pharaoh came into power, and he didn't like the fact that the Egyptians would soon be outnumbered. *This could become a real problem,* he must have thought. So he made an executive decision. He decreed that any male born to an Israelite woman would be put to death.

That's where the "basket floating down the Nile River" story began. Of course, as you already know, an Egyptian princess found Moses in the river and adopted him. As a result, Moses was raised as royalty and was groomed for leadership. Moses thrived in this setting for forty years. He received the same educational opportunities as his royal peers.

Historians tell us that Moses had years of military experience in the Egyptian Army. Early manuscripts, used by the Jewish historian, Josephus, present intriguing information about the early years of Moses.

Josephus wrote about Moses as an Egyptian prince leading an army into battle against the Ethiopians. Many other sources tell us that Moses led numerous battles over a span of ten years. Moses was obviously equipped for leadership in significant ways.

But some bad stuff happened. During his time in Egypt, Moses killed another Egyptian for beating a Hebrew man. When the word got out that Moses had killed the man, he ran for his life and spent the next forty years in the desert. Moses—the great leader—found himself leading nothing but sheep.

One lonely, desert day, God appeared to Moses in a burning bush. God told Moses He was sending him back to Egypt to tell Pharaoh to give freedom to the Hebrews. Moses fought with God about this. We told you earlier about all the excuses Moses made. But God knew he had the right man for the job. Moses had been trained to lead large groups of people, and he was also well equipped for the battles ahead. After much argument, Moses agreed with God to go to Pharaoh—and ultimately lead the Israelites out of Egypt.

Not only was Moses equipped for the difficult journey, he was also fully prepared to mentor other leaders, most prominently young Joshua. The first time we meet Joshua is in Exodus 17. The people of Israel had left Egypt, but during their journey they had to go to war with the Amalekites . . . not a nice group of people.

Moses chose Joshua to be the leader of the army in that battle. But there was a little problem. Joshua had actually been a slave from birth. He was not a general, and he hadn't been trained in the art of war. All he really knew how to do was make bricks for the Egyptian empire.

Yet, Moses (with God's advice) had *identified a suitable follower,* someone he believed he could mentor. As a trained general in the Egyptian army, Moses understood that to be successful, he would have to mentor other potential leaders who were available to serve.

Moses was an effective mentor because he taught his follower, Joshua, everything he knew.

Moses began this journey with Joshua. Joshua became his right-hand man. Moses didn't develop Joshua in the classroom, but in the trenches of leadership. This battle would be the first time Joshua would be called on to lead. The basic idea was that Joshua would fight the battle on the ground while Moses would be on top of the mountain with his staff—a strong rod or stick—raised toward God.

During the battle, as long as Moses held his staff in the air the Israelites seemed to be winning the battle. But every time Moses got tired of holding the stick in the air, his hand would drop to his side . . . and the Israelites would begin to lose the battle. Joshua learned a great lesson in the battle from Moses. "When I am dependent on God, I will win the battle. But when I am dependent on my own strength, I will lose."

Moses was an effective mentor because *he taught his follower, Joshua, everything he knew.* Joshua learned powerful lessons from Moses in the trenches of leadership. Here are a couple of examples:

On his way to receive the Ten Commandments from God, Moses took Joshua with him to the base of the mountain. During this time, Joshua was learning about the reality and the power of the God they served. As he stood at the base of the mountain, he learned from Moses about honoring God and he also learned the valuable lesson that God is not "distant"—that there is not a great chasm between the seen and unseen world.

Moses selected Joshua to become one of the twelve spies who would be sent into the Promised Land and come back with a report. Out of the twelve spies, Joshua and Caleb were the only spies who came back with a good report. Joshua was learning to believe for great things in the face of adversity.

Even though Moses didn't side with him, Joshua was learning a valuable lesson from this experience—that the majority isn't always right and that God will keep His promises. Naturally, many of the lessons Joshua learned were taught by Moses directly. But many were not.

Mentoring from the trenches is more about "doing life together" to accomplish a great goal. Much of what Joshua learned was caught more than it was taught. Joshua learned great leadership skills from Moses, but he also learned what not to do. While he learned to believe God no matter what people said, he also learned not to let the complaints of the people alter his resolve. He also learned to be a great warrior and how to command an army.

All of these lessons prepared Joshua for the mission ahead. Moses would soon die, and the baton of leadership would pass to Joshua. Moses didn't know the exact moment he would die, but he knew he had to do what every mentor has to do: *He had to turn his work over to the follower—at the right time.* Where Moses left off, Joshua picked up. He became a great general and led the Israelites to the Promised Land.

Great leaders understand there is no ongoing success without a successor. Moses found his successor in Joshua, who ultimately led the Israelites into the land promised to them by God. Former

Philippines president Gloria Macapagal-Arroyo once said, "I sow, my successor reaps. This is the majesty of democracy."[7] Servant leaders understand the importance of developing an environment in which their successors are primed for greater success and achievement than they themselves were able to accomplish.

Here's the key point. You may not live long enough to see your goals fulfilled. So you need to become a mentor to those who will see them fulfilled.

Dr. Martin Luther King's dream could have died on that day in April, 1968, when he was assassinated. But he was a mentor to his many loyal and well-trained followers who said, "We have a dream, too. It was your dream . . . and now it's our dream!"

Rich likes to share the story of the most significant mentor in his life—his dad.

. . .

I really believe that the best mentors are usually the product of good mentoring themselves. Of course, there is often an exception to every rule, but this principle is generally valid.

In my case, my mentor in life was my dad, John M. Wilkerson. He was my hero among heroes. He never stopped amazing me. I've never known another individual who better exemplifies the line, "It's not about me."

My father was much more excited by other people's wins than he ever was about his. He was the greatest promoter of other people's victories I have ever met. And he was a man's man. Young men loved hanging out with him because he exhibited every one of the servant leader's traits we've discussed in this book. He was so unlike most people that it made him highly in demand.

I'm not sure if it was a Father's Day or his birthday or what the occasion was, but about twenty-five years ago I felt a need to write an article for a magazine entitled "A Letter to the Greatest Man on Earth." It was for my dad . . . my mentor.

As you read this letter, please know that my dad is currently in his eighties and is battling dementia, but he knows Mom and me when we look into his eyes. His smile somehow still says, "I'm always on your side."

A LETTER TO THE GREATEST MAN ON EARTH

Rich Wilkerson

"O righteous Father, the world hath not known thee: but I have known thee, and these have known that thou hast sent me. And I have declared unto them thy name, and will declare it: that the love wherewith thou hast loved me may be in them, and I in them." (John 17:25–26 KJV)

Dear Dad,

I'm flying home today from meetings to be with Robyn and the boys. You can't believe how much I miss them when I'm gone. As I thought of being with Jonfulton and Richie and how much I love them, I couldn't help but think of you, Dad. It's hard to believe that there are dads in the world who don't love their kids, but I can honestly say that was never a problem for you.

You never were one to write letters or send cards, but one time you did and I'll never forget it. It was when our high school football team drove two hours to Beloit for a Friday night game. I hadn't seen you that day and had to leave with the team early in the afternoon. That weekend was a busy one for you as the pastor of our church, because it was the beginning of our missions convention. Some of the missionaries had already arrived for the weekend meeting.

That night, our team got killed! I ran back three kick-offs and never reached the twenty-yard line once. All night long that big, huge 220-pound full-back ran over me at my middle-linebacker post, and when I did make a touchdown, it was too late to make any difference. We were dejected. We'd been soundly defeated. The bus trip home was long and quiet as we nursed our wounds. I suppose I got home from the trip about 2:00 a.m. The lights were out and everyone was in bed. I headed downstairs to my basement bedroom.

When I turned on the light, there was a note from you on my bed. You had been at the game! You had driven all the way to Beloit! You had even coaxed one of the poor missionaries into enduring the trip and the game with you.

As I read the note I started to cry. You wrote about how proud you were of me and what an incredible series of kick-off returns I had made, and how sore that full-back would be the next morning after all the hits I'd put on him, and how that was one of the greatest touchdown runs you'd ever seen. You told me not to worry about losing, because I had done my best.

I guess I was crying, Dad, because I figured that if you had been to that game, in which we had been creamed, and came away with a proud feeling for your son, it was only because you loved me. You overlooked my failure and only saw my good. THANKS, DAD!

Dad, I don't know if I ever told you this before, but when I was about fifteen, I was struggling because we didn't have much money. The church furnished us with a house and a car, but beyond that, we didn't have a lot of extras, and it used to burn me. The reason I'd get upset was because I knew there were some very well-to-do people who attended our church and I figured they were pretty tight with the purse strings, when it came to the pastor's salary.

One day I cornered Mr. Hartnell, who was my favorite Sunday school teacher of all time, as well as the church treasurer and a deacon. I said, "Mr. Hartnell, what's the deal? We've got all kinds of money in this church; how come you guys are choking our family financially?"

He sat down and said, "Well, son, the church pays most of your family's expenses and we give your mom and dad $8,000 per year as a salary." At that time (late sixties) that was a fair middle-income salary. Mr. Hartnell then said, "Rich, I'm the church treasurer and I know that your dad gave almost half of that salary back to the church last year!"

Dad, I couldn't believe it. At first I was mad at you for giving all of our money back to the church. But there was a little line you used to always tell me: "You can't out-give God." That has been imprinted on my life. I thought back and realized that we had never gone without food or shelter or clothing. I knew that God had always met our needs. You know what I did? I went out and got a job at a gas station so that I could start giving to God. In so doing, God gave me some things I had complained about not having earlier.

When Robyn and I felt that God wanted us to start traveling as missionaries to young people, we had no salary or support of any kind. You and Mom believed in what God had called us to do. From the very beginning, you and Mom started sending monthly support. Today we've grown in our organization and ministry. Hundreds of people support this missionary outreach each year. But Dad, there's never an offering that arrives in our office that means more to me than yours, because your gift represents a lifestyle. You taught me to be a giving person, Dad. Thanks!

Of course Dad, you and I will never forget the time in junior high when I changed the grade on my report card from an F to a B in citizenship. I pulled it off for a day. After that one day, I was going crazy with "Holy Spirit conviction." Remember, I called you and Mom into the living room and told you what I had done? It was one of the only times I can remember ever blatantly lying to you.

You said, "Son, go to your bedroom." I knew what that meant. I thought you were going to "wail on my fourteen-year-old tail" for sure. I was in my room sitting on the bed, waiting . . . waiting . . . waiting. The waiting was always the toughest part.

That particular day was to be different than all the other times that I faced punishment for my wrong actions. On that day, Dad, you walked into my room and you didn't have a "paddle". You sat down in the big green chair, you put your head in your hands, and you just cried and cried.

As I watched you cry, Dad, I cried, too, because I knew how much I had hurt you. I thought for just a few moments that God was sitting right next to you crying also. The longer I live, the more I'm convinced He was. I wanted you to paddle me. I wanted to pay for my sin; I was truly sorry.

That day, after you dried your eyes, you looked at me and said, "Son, I'll not be paddling you anymore, because today you've started your trek toward manhood. From now on, you'll have to give an account to God. Son, I want you to know that when you sin, you break your heavenly Father's heart. He loves you, Rich, and He wants your life to go well. Sin will ruin you. Live for God!' Dad, you showed me the broken heart of Father God. You showed me how God longs for His children to do right so that life will go well for them. I'll never forget it. Thanks!

One more thing Dad; I'm sure you have forgotten, but you made me go back to my history teacher, my homeroom teacher, and Mr. Young, the principal. You made me apologize to each one of them for lying about my grade and admit that with God's help I'd never do it again. Wow, that was tough, but Dad, you taught me to be a man of integrity! Thanks!

Dad, the verses that I started this letter with are the words Christ prayed to His Father. The line that gets me is, "O righteous Father, the world hath not known thee: but I have known thee."

That's the way I feel today. I read the papers and I see the news and I also know the people whom the world calls great. Sometimes I just want to stand up in front of the whole world and say, "Hey, you should know John Wilkerson!" Because if the world knew you like I know you, Dad, the presidents and the kings of this earth would have to step aside.

If the cycle of life stands true in the Wilkerson family, as it generally has for other families throughout the course of time, you will probably see Jesus before I do.

I just wanted you to know that I'm not into eulogies. I'm into living memorials. That's what this letter has been about. A man named Fogelberg wrote the following words about his father. These words best express how I feel about you, Dad. The song is called, "Leader of the Band."

He left his home and went his lone and solitary way
and he gave to me a gift I know I never can repay.

He earned his love through discipline, a thundering velvet hand,

his gentle means of sculpting souls took me years to understand.

I thank you for your music and your stories of the road.

I thank you for the freedom when it came my time to go.

I thank you for the kindness and the times when you got tough.

And Poppa, I don't think I said "I love you" near enough.

The leader of the band is tired and his eyes are growing old,

but his blood runs through my message and his song is in my soul.

My life has been a poor attempt to imitate the man.

I'm just a living legacy to the leader of the band.

I guess the reason why I'm so in love with my heavenly Father today is because He gave me an earthly father who is just like Him. This brings me back to the topic of my own boys. I can't predict whether or not they will ever love me as much as I love you, Dad, but I know this, that because of you, I'll be able to love them as much as you love me. Well, the plane just touched down. Gotta go.

Love,
Rich

P. S. Tell Mom I'll write her as soon as possible. You didn't think I would forget her, did you?

That's the power of mentoring! There's also great power in expressing gratitude to your mentors for what they have contributed to your life!

REFLECTION QUESTIONS

1. Have you had or do you have a mentor in your life?

2. Has your role as a servant leader been shaped by a mentor? In what ways did your mentor teach, coach, engage, praise, and correct you?

3. Are you mentoring someone to take over your leadership role?

ACTION SUGGESTION

If you are not involved in a mentoring role, either as a mentor or as a person being mentored, consider it!

CHAPTER SIXTEEN

FLEXIBILITY

*"Let no one think that flexibility and a predisposition
to compromise is a sign of weakness or a sell-out."*
—PAUL KAGAME (PRESIDENT OF RWANDA)

COULD IT BE THAT THE REASON our government frequently
gets embroiled in gridlock is because neither side wants to be flexible?

It appears that everyone involved wants it all his or her way.
There is no compromise . . . no giving in . . . no consideration of
opposing views. Both sides somehow think that if they compromise,
they are selling out their values or, worse yet, their vision.

It seems to us that it is in those times when all parties are
willing to be flexible that the most good happens. Flexibility has
proven to be a good thing in the past.

President Ronald Reagan and Speaker of the House Tip
O'Neill disagreed on a number of ideas, policies, and their overall
view of the world. Yet, at the end of the day, after most members

of Congress had gone home for the night, Reagan, a Republican, and O'Neill, a Democrat, would get together socially and discuss ideas and feelings and beliefs—the kinds of things that great people feel free to discuss. Though there will always be those who disagree with our observation, we believe their flexibility led to the resolution of many important issues.

Going back even further in history, President Abraham Lincoln also had a servant leader's view of flexibility. In the mid-1800s, the United States found itself in one of the most trying times in our young history. Slavery was an issue that caused a bitter division within our nation. The country was essentially divided along geographical lines. The Southern states wanted to preserve slavery, while the Northern states wanted it abolished.

In 1858, through a series of political debates, a very unlikely leader made himself highly visible to the public due to his stance on slavery. Abraham Lincoln believed all men should be free.

Few people believed Lincoln had a chance to win when he ran for office as the Republican Party nominee. Among his best-known opponents was a charismatic man by the name of William H. Seward. Yet, after a long and fierce campaign, Abraham Lincoln became the sixteenth president of the United States. Though the journey to the presidency was long and hard, the real battle had just begun.

When the new president took office, seven states from the South declared secession from the Union, starting a bitter journey toward the Civil War. During this time, President Lincoln chose not to focus on the states that were leaving the Union, but instead focused on choosing his cabinet members. He understood that if he was going to succeed in keeping the states united he needed capable people beside him for the journey.

Many leaders in this situation would have immediately searched for people who were like-minded and believed in the same exact principles. However, this wasn't the case for Abraham Lincoln! He displayed the servant leader's trait of flexibility and appointed cabinet members who were previously his rivals.

For example, he named his opponent in the race for the presidency—William H. Seward—as his Secretary of State. Differences and disagreements didn't stop Lincoln from doing what he felt was necessary. He understood the need for flexibility and continued to place people with differing beliefs and values in key positions.

Despite their many differences, Lincoln and his cabinet members did agree on one thing—they all recognized that saving the Union was more important than their individual positions on many other issues. Lincoln took advantage of this common ground, and he began to build his team.

Using the influence of his cabinet members, together they united several of the states for the long war that was quickly approaching. From the beginning, it was Lincoln's vision to build a team made up of both Republicans and Democrats. Knowing they had very different viewpoints, he knew they were all flexible enough to give their all to save our nation. Because of this, he was able to lead the country through perhaps its darkest hours.

That road was not easy. The Civil War was the most devastating war, in terms of casualties, that the United States had ever endured. But Lincoln was able to keep the Union alive. It's not necessary to

> **"**
> It's not necessary to see everything eye-to-eye, but it is vital to share a common purpose and vision.

see everything eye-to-eye, but it is vital to share a common purpose and vision. That's the power of flexibility. Lincoln recognized in 1858 what Gary Yukl and Richard Lepsinger are still teaching today. "Successful adaptation in a turbulent environment usually requires flexibility and innovation. In this situation, leaders are expected to be visionary reformers and agents of change, not defenders of tradition."[1]

We'll never forget January 12, 2010, for as long as we live. At approximately 4:50 p.m. that afternoon, a 7.0 magnitude earthquake hit Léogane, Haiti, sixteen miles west of Port-au-Prince. Some three million people were affected by this tragedy. The highest death count tabulated by international organizations was 220,000, but Haiti's government estimates were considerably higher—250,000 lives lost.

More than 200,000 homes were destroyed, and 30,000 commercial buildings collapsed or were severely damaged. Landmarks including the Presidential Palace, The National Assembly, and the Port-au-Prince Cathedral were all destroyed. It happened on a Tuesday. As we mentioned earlier in the book, Tuesdays are Vous Day @trinitymiami.

At least 1,100 young adults gather every week for a celebration like no other. But that Tuesday was different. With half of our congregation being of Haitian descent, young adults began streaming to the church within thirty minutes of the announcement, two hours before our normally scheduled meeting. They came into the sanctuary and knelt and began to sob with an anguish that we never want to hear again.

It was an unusual Vous gathering to say the least. The following night, we had a citywide prayer meeting for Haiti, and the news agencies were there. Flexibility was the name of the game at that time. With all the other obligations we had as an organization, we all realized we could do so much more when pressed into duty.

In subsequent months, we made four trips with different teams from our church to assess not only the damage, but ways we could help. We were able to secure a ship from the Friend Ships organization out of Port Mercy in Lake Charles, Louisiana, and permission from the Port of Miami and the Longshoremen's Union President, to allow our ship to travel back and forth between Miami and Haiti with emergency supplies for six months—at no charge. Trinity Broadcasting Network paid for all the fuel for the ship, and the longshoremen of Miami volunteered all of their time to load the ship.

This had never been done in their history, but it happened then. Why? Flexibility. Tragedy had hit our beloved Haiti, and in that difficult time, rules changed. People's schedules didn't matter . . . time seemed to stand still.

Servant leadership principles took over to see a nation touched with love. In our own congregation, we identified 400 people who had lost an immediate family member in the earthquake. Can you imagine the impact of an organization or church having a funeral for 400 at one time?

The impact was excruciating. According to Steve Echols and Allan England, "The presence of a crisis event or circumstance intensifies the leadership challenge and spotlights the leader and the leadership moment. Crises accentuate the dynamics of leadership and reveal a leader's strengths and weaknesses in a way that ordinary challenges do not."[2] In the midst of the pain, suffering, and anguish, servant leaders of every description, age, race, religion, and work background determined that they would become as flexible as humanly possible. "I'll do what I have to in order to bring about a victory for a broken nation," was their resolve.

This same resolve—this same willingness to be flexible—was described by the apostle Paul. He seemed to face disaster on a never-ending basis, but here's what he said in 2 Corinthians 4:8–12, 16–18:

> *We've been surrounded and battered by troubles, but we're not demoralized; we're not sure what to do, but we know that God knows what to do; we've been spiritually terrorized, but God hasn't left our side; we've been thrown down, but we haven't broken. What they did to Jesus, they do to us—trial and torture, mockery and murder; what Jesus did among them, he does in us—he lives! Our lives are at constant risk for Jesus' sake, which makes Jesus' life all the more evident in us. While we're going through the worst, you're getting in on the best!*
>
> *So we're not giving up. How could we! Even though on the outside it often looks like things are falling apart on us, on the inside, where God is making new life, not a day goes by without his unfolding grace. These hard times are small potatoes compared to the coming good times, the lavish celebration prepared for us. There's far more here than meets the eye. The things we see now are here today, gone tomorrow. But the things we can't see now will last forever.*

Flexibility is an essential quality in all servant leaders, however it's only accomplished when they are both humble and committed to their vision. Jim Collins supports this notion in his bestselling leadership book, *Good to Great*. According to Collins, great leaders are humble. When things go well, they look out and give everybody else the credit. However when things go wrong, they look in the mirror and ask themselves "What could I have done differently to allow these people to be as great as they could be?"[3]

A genuine servant leader is committed to the ultimate goal of serving others and, as such, is willing to compromise their approach for the achievement of the cause. This doesn't mean servant leaders must compromise on their values or principles, rather they must have the humility and courage to work with others to accomplish a task. "Flexibility should not be confused with practicing a 'laissez faire' style of leadership in which the leader's engagement in the form of guidance, direction, and organization is lacking. The flexible leader is fully engaged in a sensitive, proactive and responsive way."[4]

We've discovered that the trait of flexibility empowers leaders to give up opinions that often restrain, while holding fast to the underlying goals that make a difference to a hurting world.

REFLECTION QUESTIONS

1. Crisis can make or break a leader. What leadership "wins" can you recall during a major crisis? What did that leader do to successfully guide their team and others involved in the crisis?

2. Great loss is a horrible hardship for any organization to bear, not least because every heart hurts together. This is a time when servant leaders lay aside all differences and work together to help everyone heal.

Can you recall a situation when this has occurred in your life? How did you react to the situation?

3. Flexibility is key for a servant leader, especially in times of crisis. What are some of the ways you are flexible as a servant leader?

ACTION SUGGESTION

Make a list of situations in which you have had a difficult time being flexible. Beside each, write how you could have handled the situation in a more flexible way.

CHAPTER SEVENTEEN

RESILIENCE

"The real test in golf and in life is not in keeping out of the rough, but in getting out after you are in."

—ZIG ZIGLAR

THERE IS A STORY-TELLING technique that is employed in nearly every movie you've ever seen—or ever will see. If you don't know about it already, it will become obvious to you after you read about it here.

This technique is called "the apparent defeat."

Without going into too much movie-making detail, most movies are about a main character (the hero or protagonist) who wants something, and the people who don't want that person to get it. This is the age-old conflict between the hero and the villain (antagonist), or between good and evil.

In most movies, the hero is living an ordinary life when something pivotal happens to thrust him or her into a new situation. This is called the "inciting incident" or "plot point one," and it usually happens early in the story.

In *Star Wars*, Luke Skywalker's adopted parents are killed, and since he no longer has a reason to stay at home, he follows his new friend, Obi-Wan Kenobi, into a new life of adventure and peril . . . pursuing the call of Princess Leia, which appeared to him in a hologram projected by R2D2. (Some film buffs feel the hologram image of Princess Leia projected by R2D2 is actually plot point one.)

In movie terms, when plot point one happens, act two begins. This is the longest part of the typical three-act movie, in which additional characters are introduced (including Darth Vader, the villain; and Han Solo, Luke's primary ally) and the hero encounters all sorts of challenges, difficulties, and setbacks. Among other things, the Death Star becomes operational and destroys an entire peaceful planet, our gang is captured and faces death, Obi Wan Kenobi is vanquished in a light saber battle, and Han Solo abandons Luke just as the good guys are about to attack the Death Star in an attempt to destroy it.

But Luke and the Princess keep bouncing back. They demonstrate irrepressible resilience.

The moment of apparent defeat, also known as plot point two, comes when the Death Star is in range of the rebel base, most of the rebel fighter pilots have been shot down, and Vader is in hot pursuit of Luke—his guns locked in on the only one who has a chance to destroy the Death Star. But Han has a change of heart, returns to the battle, and gets a direct shot at Vader's space ship, allowing Luke to get off the direct hit that destroys the battle station. End of movie.

If you're a Star Wars fan, you know the story well. If not, you now know more than you probably ever wanted to know. The point is, in this movie, as in most other movies and novels, the hero generally emerges from apparent defeat to achieve his or her goal.

As we noted, we often call this trait *resilience*. We like to refer to it as the "bounce back." "Some people are resilient even in extremely stressful circumstances. They turn disruptive changes and conflicts from potential disasters into growth opportunities."[1]

The dramatic elements we've just described come into play in one of the most intriguing stories from history—the story of Joseph. You can find the biblical account in the book of Genesis, and you may have even seen the hit Broadway musical, *Joseph and the Amazing Technicolor Dreamcoat.*

Joseph was one of twelve sons of a guy named Jacob, and he somehow became his dad's favorite. We're not sure if it was because he was smarter or better looking than the rest, but when it came to working around the homestead, he got off easy, probably because Joseph was born when Jacob was quite old, so it seems that the other brothers had to do the "heavy lifting."

Dad also decided to have a fancy, colorful embroidered coat made for his prized son . . . and Joseph decided it was his job to flaunt it. In fact, Joseph got such a big head that he told his brothers he had a dream in which they would one day bow down to him. Naturally, the other brothers were thoroughly annoyed. "We have to do something about this," they schemed.

One day, Jacob decided to send Joseph out to the fields to check on his brothers, who were tending to their father's sheep. When the older brothers saw Joseph approach, they were delighted, "Perfect! Let's ditch the kid." So they threw him into a pit to die. "We'll just tell Dad the wild animals got him."

Then, one of the more pragmatic brothers made a suggestion: "Let's at least turn the kid into cash. Let's sell him as a slave. We can still tell Dad he was food for animals."

"Done deal," the other brothers agreed.

Off Joseph went with slave traders, and he ended up in Egypt. And there you have the "inciting incident," or plot point one.

Now, again, from a movie perspective, this is the beginning of act two. This act is packed with ups and downs, good and evil, defeat and victory. Joseph's story is certainly filled with all of that.

The slave traders who bought Joseph from his brothers sold him to a man named Potiphar, a ruler in Egypt who had a large company of slaves who worked for him.

Slavery, of course, was an enormous challenge for the favored son of Jacob. Here, Joseph's dream was challenged for the first time in a powerful way. He had a choice to allow his change in status to cause him to feel sorry for himself, or he could strive to rise above the struggle. Either way, at this point, we're fairly certain he had serious doubts that his brothers would ever bow to him. "Scratch that dream," he must have said to himself.

Joseph quickly made up his mind that he would not be a victim of his circumstances, but would make the best out of his situation. He decided to embrace his struggle by becoming the best servant leader he could be.

At this point, Joseph had no status to fall back on; no glorious, multicolored coat; and no father offering him the easy life. So he chose to serve Potiphar with all of his heart.

Almost immediately, Potiphar began to see there was something different about this servant. He didn't have to harass him or demand more or better of him. Joseph always gave 100 percent and could be trusted.

Potiphar began to think highly of Joseph, and, over time, Joseph became the chief servant in Potiphar's house. Through the power of servanthood, Joseph rose from lowly slave to become the number one person Potiphar relied on to get things done.

Joseph was beginning to realize that a true servant leader will grow in favor with everyone around him. He had made the decision to bounce back from a trying situation by serving the people around him.

Remember, though, that we said act two is filled with ups and downs, and victories and setbacks.

Potiphar was married to a woman who thought that Joseph was one good looking guy. She watched every move he made, in the meantime making several passes at him. Her lust for Joseph was starting to get out of control.

One day she caught Joseph alone in the house and begged him to have sex with her. Joseph's integrity was now on the line. In that instant, Joseph made a decision that would change everything for him. Instead of sleeping with Potiphar's wife, he decided to run from her.

While he was leaving, she grabbed his robe, tore it away, and left him practically naked. She was likely both angry and embarrassed that she still had Joseph's robe in her hand, so she made up a story that Joseph tried to rape her—and told Potiphar the entire fabricated story. Naturally angry, Potiphar had Joseph thrown in prison.

Joseph must have thought; "My brothers were bad enough, and now this!" It seemed that all his hard work had been for nothing. He had gone from bad to worse. Nothing was going right for him.

There's an important theme emerging from Joseph's story. All servant leaders will go through trying times. How they respond to these trying times becomes the measure of their greatness—and their faithfulness. In *Resilient Leadership for Turbulent Times,* the authors state, "We define a resilient leader as a person who demonstrates the ability to recover, learn from, and developmentally mature when confronted by chronic or crisis adversity."[2]

Joseph met their qualities of a resilient leader. He chose to do what he had always done. He would become the best servant he could be in the situation he was in. Before long, Joseph became the number one servant in the prison. He was resilient. He bounced back yet again. While in prison, through a series of events, Joseph found himself joined by two of Pharaoh's old servants, the cupbearer and the baker.

They each had dreams, and Joseph was able to serve them by giving them the meaning of the dreams. This act of service would pay off for Joseph in a life-changing way. In the cupbearer's dream, he was restored to power in Pharaoh's court and was again given his authority. Joseph told the cupbearer to remember him when he was returned to his former position.

Of course, another setback is part of act two. When the cupbearer was placed back in authority—just as Joseph believed he would be—he forgot about Joseph. Once again, Joseph was overlooked by everyone he had helped and served.

But one day, the Pharaoh had a dream that troubled him. He had no idea what the meaning could possibly be. The cupbearer remembered Joseph and told the Pharaoh of a man in prison named Joseph who would likely be able to give him the meaning of his dream.

Now, imagine this: If Joseph had not had a servant's heart in prison, he would not have helped the cupbearer and would have missed the great opportunity God had for him.

> All servant leaders will go through trying times. How they respond to these trying times becomes the measure of their greatness—and their faithfulness.

The Pharaoh commanded his men to bring Joseph to his courts. Here was Joseph, a favored son, sold into slavery by his brothers, wrongfully convicted of rape, who was now standing before the most powerful man on earth . . . all because he had the heart to bounce back and serve.

Joseph then gave the Pharaoh the interpretation of his dream. The Pharaoh was astounded by Joseph's wisdom and appointed him to a major leadership position in his kingdom.

The Pharaoh's prophetic dream revealed two things. First, that there would be seven years of prosperity. Farmers would produce bumper crops and there would be abundance throughout Egypt. Second, that the abundance would be followed by seven years of crop failures and famine. Egypt would face difficult years ahead.

The Pharaoh didn't really know how to respond to the coming famine, but he decided to place his trust in the wisdom of Joseph to lead the empire through this trying time. Joseph became the second in command in Egypt to guide the nation through the coming troubled times.

So far in our "movie," a young man from a foreign land had been sold into slavery, was unjustly accused and sent to prison, and then became the second most powerful leader in the world. That's a story of resilience! That's the "bounce back" in action!

Joseph never allowed his situation to control him. He always assumed the role of a servant and made the best of every situation. All of his service was now positioning him to fulfill his dreams and destiny.

Back in Joseph's homeland, the famine that hit Egypt also devastated Israel, where Dad and the brothers and their families lived. But rumors circulated that there was plenty of food in neighboring Egypt. So Dad decided that his family's only hope was to turn to Egypt for help—and he sent his sons on a long journey to obtain food.

When Joseph's brothers arrived in Egypt, they bowed before him and begged him for food. Joseph was overwhelmed with emotion, and told them he would help them on one condition: they would have to bring their youngest brother, Benjamin, back to appear before him.

Of course, in movie fashion, he originally never told the brothers who he was—and they certainly didn't recognize him.

On their return visit, Joseph finally revealed his identity to his family. He sent his brothers back to Israel with their sacks full of grain, and told them to come live in Egypt. Dad, desperate to see his presumed-dead son, joined them on the long journey. Naturally, father and son wept long and hard when they were reunited.

In that moment, Joseph realized the fulfillment of his dream. The truth was, his dream was never about him being the ruler of his family; it was about him serving his family. He now realized God had sent him to Egypt ahead of his family to save them during a time of great trial.

The fulfillment of Joseph's dream was overwhelming to everyone involved. Joseph was now the second most powerful man on the earth, and he was reunited with his family. That's the power of bouncing back through trying situations. It's how the dreams of servant leaders are fulfilled.

> Joseph exhibited the proper response to life's surprises and serendipity; he was resilient in the face of adversity and, as a result, excelled in every bend of his journey.

Former Secretary of State, Condoleezza Rice once said "Life is full of surprises and serendipity. Being open to unexpected turns in the road is an important part of success. If you try to plan every step, you may miss those wonderful twists and turns. Just find your next adventure, do it well, enjoy it, and then think about what comes next."[3] Joseph exhibited the proper response to life's surprises and serendipity; he was resilient in the face of adversity and, as a result, excelled in every bend of his journey.

You may be asking, "Where is the apparent defeat in this story?"

The simple answer is that this story is the story of many apparent defeats. But unlike the typical movie script, it's really the story of the ultimate, complete victory! It's the story of what happens in the life of a faithful servant leader.

The lessons that apply to servant leadership aren't limited to stories from history. In fact, we personally know a woman from today who exemplifies the servant leader's trait of resilience—of the ability to bounce back.

Her name is Cynthia Strickland.

Cynthia was raised in a large family. Her parents had no interest in God, so she was brought up with no church background whatsoever. By the time she was nineteen, she was married and had her first son, Brian.

The dad of the family wasn't there for either Mom or son. She had to do it all on her own. It was a difficult life, but she determined that she would be resilient. The marriage eventually ended in divorce—not of her choosing, but because she had simply run out of options in her life.

About that time, Cynthia somehow sensed a need for a relationship with God, and she became a Christian at age twenty-eight. She immediately got immersed in service at Trinity Church, which is where we eventually met her.

She remarried and had two more children. Her oldest son was a real trooper at age twelve, and he helped care for his younger siblings. But she was again neglected and ignored by her husband, and another divorce ensued.

Always the resilient woman, Cynthia woke up one morning and said to herself, "I have to make something better of my life." She earned her undergraduate degree—all while working full-time and raising three children alone—and in 1993, she was accepted to law school at Barry University in Miami.

Life as a law student was extremely difficult for Cynthia. She worked forty hours a week for a law firm, went to school at night, studied almost until the dawn of the next day, and then started the cycle all over again. Amazingly, she still had the time and energy to focus attention on her children. But this faithful servant was forced to miss years of service at Trinity. There were simply no more hours in her days or her weeks. Yet she lived this demanding life for three and a half years!

Cynthia graduated from law school in 1996, and, after a long struggle, finally found a job with a law firm that was willing to take a chance on a woman. Female attorneys—especially if they were African American—found very few open doors back then. But she ultimately got a job. Resilience and perseverance do pay off.

In 2004, Cynthia decided to strike out on her own. As a true servant leader, Cynthia recognized that there are many people in our community—especially in the geographical area surrounding Trinity Church—who don't have the means to be represented by expensive legal counsel.

So Cynthia abandoned the idea of a grand office with mahogany paneling and an impressive conference room lined with law books, and instead set up her law firm in her home. Today, she meets with clients in her car, at a Starbucks, or in a city park. She specializes in civil litigation, personal injury, family law, and contract law. Thanks to laptop computers and the Internet, she can be mobile and go where the people need her. She is truly a "street lawyer"—the kind John Grisham wrote about in one of his bestselling novels.

While it can be a challenge for Cynthia to get paid, she does everything with an attitude of service. It's the most important thing to her—more important than money. Cynthia Strickland would tell you that she has a wonderful life! Her children have all achieved successful lives, she helps others through her education and skills, and she is a faithful servant in her church—our church! She says that serving others sustains her and gives her joy, and that big smile on her face proves it. In fact, on a typical Saturday evening, you can find our resilient "street lawyer" serving popcorn in our lobby before our Saturday service!

The stories of Joseph and Cynthia illustrate the power of the "bounce back." When life gives us trying situations, they become our opportunity to overcome. Our most overwhelming trials can become our greatest triumphs. Our apparent defeats can become our biggest victories.

Servant leaders view obstacles and setbacks as essential growth opportunities to effectively serve those they were called to lead. In his memoir, *A Twentieth Century Testimony*, English author and journalist, Malcolm Muggeridge shares:

> I can say with complete truthfulness that everything I have learned in my seventy-five years in this world, everything that has truly enhanced and enlightened my existence, has been through affliction and not through happiness, whether pursued or attained. In other words, if it ever were to be possible to eliminate affliction from our earthly existence by means of some drug or other medical mumbo jumbo . . . the result would not be to make life delectable, but to make it too banal and trivial to be endurable.[4]

What Muggeridge has wisely articulated is that what seem to be insurmountable obstacles or challenges will cultivate the qualities and endurance necessary to live a life of meaning and purpose.

As servant leaders, we must make the decision to bounce back when life's trials come up against our dreams or our circumstances.

If you make this decision, you will not only see your dreams come true, but will also see the dreams of many others come true. Resilience is an essential trait of the effective servant leader!

REFLECTION QUESTIONS

1. Have you experienced a "plot point one" or "inciting incident"? What challenges, difficulties, and setbacks did it lead to?

2. When you encounter a moment of apparent defeat, especially as a servant leader, how do you react? Do you respond with resilience?

3. Joseph and Cynthia both worked hard to bounce back and to serve others with great joy. How does this process work in your life? Have you bounced back from a difficult situation as a servant leader?

ACTION SUGGESTION

Think of attitudes, procedures, and support systems that will help you bounce back from any future trial. Implement those you can and put the others in your resiliency arsenal. Keep adding to it as time goes on, and share it with others around you. Become the resilient servant leader we know you can be!

CHAPTER EIGHTEEN

SELFLESSNESS

—

"Only a life lived for others is worth living."
—ALBERT EINSTEIN

THIS WAS A CHALLENGING chapter for us to think about, and to write. The reason is that many, if not most, of the traits of a servant leader involve selflessness.

For example, a servant leader's *vision* has to do with the ways in which he or she wants to serve. "How will the world be changed for the better by what I do?" Throughout history, a selfless vision has always been the most powerful.

A servant leader's *values* are the driving force behind every single action. The effective leader deliberately chooses values that are selfless. As an example, generosity is not only a trait of the servant leader. It is also a selfless value. "Servant leaders motivate through modeling and proclaiming the importance of service for the sake of others."[1] They do this by sharing their values with others.

Faithfulness often, if not always, involves selflessness. It means you turn your back on your own desires to become faithful to another . . . to their cause. It doesn't, however, mean you abandon your own dreams or goals. Faithfulness almost always involves creating meaningful partnerships.

For example, as a married couple, we are faithful to each other and to our children. We are a partnership in marriage. We still have our individual goals, but they don't interfere with our faithfulness.

Acceptance is another trait of a selfless servant leader. When we were writing about Graham earlier, it was painful for us to realize that many parents of so-called special needs children don't fully accept those children. They feel disappointed—that they were somehow "let down" by the "gods."

"We don't deserve to be in this situation," they say.

We wish we had the extra pages we would need to tell you the stories of people we know whose lives were enriched—and whose lives became a true blessing to others—because of the way they accepted cancer, or infertility, or the death of a loved one. Acceptance is more than an important trait; it's an amazing gift! It's a selfless way to live life!

Loyalty is often the ultimate example of selflessness. Think about the servicemen and servicewomen who died on battlefields, in the skies, or on the seas because of their loyalty to their countries; not just our country, but nations all over the world. Sometimes their loyalty is misplaced—because their cause is misguided or unjust. But their loyalty endures.

A true servant leader is aligned with just causes and goals.

Humility is selfless, because, at its core, it is saying "You come first . . . I come second. Or last."

There's certainly nothing wrong with being self-confident or self-assured. The problem surfaces when we become self-centered or egotistical, when our ego dictates our behaviors. Ken Blanchard has described ego as "Edging God Out."[2] True servant leaders cannot perceive themselves as "gods." Rather, they humble themselves before God and people.

The selfless servant leader has *integrity*. The desire to keep one's word, even if doing so turns out to be "inconvenient," is a clear sign of selflessness.

Compassion is closely aligned with *generosity*. Compassion is that voice in your mind and heart that tells you what to do for others; generosity is the ever-unfolding and ongoing action behind the voice.

> **"**
>
> There's certainly nothing wrong with being self-confident or self-assured. The problem surfaces when we become self-centered or egotistical.

Encouragement and *respect* are likewise closely aligned traits of the selfless servant leader. Mentoring fits in this broad category, too, because it is a form of Encouragement.

Flexibility and *resilience* are mutually inclusive traits, as well. Resilience enhances a leader's flexibility. People who tend to give up easily lose their capacity for flexibility. How many people do you know who simply "check out" when they feel they can't make a comeback from a situation or set of circumstances? Giving up is actually a form of selfishness.

Ultimately, selflessness involves giving it your all. Everything. 100 percent. "The servant leader model is counterintuitive because it defies the common sense of a culture that values either self-serving individualism or selfless collectivism without understanding the concept of servant-oriented power or embracing the concept of powerful service for the common good."[3] Luckily, we have had the privilege of meeting a man who perfectly understood the value of selflessness.

Pastor O. A. Alderson was one of the most selfless people we've ever met. He was one of just a handful of Anglo people left in the original Trinity Church we came to serve in 1998. He was sixty-seven when we met him, and for thirty years, he had been a Miami firefighter. He told some of the most fascinating stories we have ever heard.

His career with the fire department ended as a result of a terrible accident during a fire on a ship in Key Biscayne Bay. O. A. was thrown off the fireboat he was working from. On his way down into the water, his ear was cut off by the propeller on the boat. They eventually pulled him out of sixty feet of water.

It's a long story, but, miraculously, his ear was restored and his brain wasn't damaged. He retired with a handsome severance and went to seminary, where he eventually received his doctorate in theology. He also became the chaplain of the Miami Fire Department—a post he held until his death in 2012.

O. A. basically spent his life at the church. In the early days, he did maintenance on his days off. He laid all the tile in the church, visited the sick, was the youth leader, and then the singles leader. He also always taught the Monday night Bible study long before there was Monday night football!

"Pastor O," as we called him, had a unique ability to attract young men who were looking for a fatherly word of advice or wisdom. We can recall so many times seeing him walk through the hallways of the church with a group of twenty somethings, laughing and teaching. That was Pastor O.

One of the young men he influenced tremendously was James Lewis. James, now thirty-five and married with a son, would spend hours listening to Pastor O offer his words of wisdom.

James has a father who loves him and has been there for him from a distance, but Pastor O was like a grandfather to him. James was quite rough around the edges. He came from a tough part of Miami, where gangs and drugs are just a part of life and growing up.

James's mother, Dr. Mary Mites, is truly one in a million. She's the lead nurse in the Dade County correctional facility hospital. She's also the first African-American woman to receive her doctorate in nursing from Barry University. She raised James as a single mother while working her way through college and living on ketchup sandwiches.

James was first hired at Trinity as one of our AmeriCorps members. When that two-year stint was completed, he became our assistant operations director, and in that time received his contractor's license. He is a selfless servant leader who will do anything for anyone at anytime! That's just James!

In the fall of 2011, Pastor Alderson was taken to the hospital with congestive heart failure. Even in the hospital, with a failing heart, his love was known to all. We'd visit him, and he couldn't speak because of a tracheotomy in his throat. But at eighty—with a smile on his face and tears coming down his cheeks—he would mouth the words "I love You" over and over again—to anyone who visited him . . . and there was a steady stream of visitors.

The Sunday he died, we received a text from Lester Mitchell, who leads our hospital visitation program, letting us know that he was at Pastor O's side and that Pastor O had just gone to heaven. We watched as the message began to spread through the audience during our worship service that Pastor O was gone. That crowd of about 750 people began to cry.

The next morning we had our weekly Monday team chapel, where about sixty of our 130 staff members gather weekly for devotions. We asked if anyone would like to come to the front and share a story about what Pastor O meant to them. The first up was James Lewis. He told a story none of us knew and none of us will ever forget.

He said he knew of a young woman thirty-four years ago who was single and eight months pregnant when her apartment was broken into and she was nearly beaten to death with a baseball bat. The intruder got what he wanted and left. The young woman, now delirious with pain, somehow called 911. When the fire truck got there, in rushed O. A. Alderson. He helped resuscitate her and get her onto the gurney. He rode with her in the truck, praying over her and continually saying, "I've got you, Ma'am." She was in the hospital for days, and each day firefighter O would come after work and encourage her and pray over her and tell her that her baby would be fine and healthy.

She recovered, and miraculously, the baby boy was born and he was perfectly normal and healthy! Fast forward twenty-seven years. One Sunday morning this same woman walked into the old Trinity Church air dome tent on Interstate 95, and as she stood at the back of the tent listening to the worship service, a man came up to her and put his arm around her shoulder and said, "I've got you, Ma'am." It was Pastor O, and the woman was the one who twenty-eight years earlier had experienced that near-death experience when then-firefighter O showed up to say, "I've got you, Ma'am."

He hadn't seen her in nearly twenty-eight years, but this selfless servant leader remembered that woman. James began to cry that morning as he said to us, "When Pastor O said, 'I've got you Ma'am,' he had me, too, because that woman is my mother, Dr. Mary Mites. And the little boy she was carrying at eight months was me." At that moment, we all somehow knew that the selfless loving servant leader that Pastor O had been would now be evident in his friend James. "I've got you!"

The same selflessness and dedication can also be present in service industries. We spend a great deal of time traveling, and as a result we spend a lot of times in hotels. In all of our travels we have learned that what makes a hotel distinctive is not the décor or architecture, what sets good hotels apart from the great is service.

Perhaps one of the greatest stories of hospitality and service in the hotel industry is the story of the historic Waldorf-Astoria in New York City. The Waldorf-Astoria is highly acclaimed for its superb customer service, which originates from its first general manager, George Boldt. The story is told that Mr. Boldt operated a small resort hotel in New Jersey, when a relative of the Astors who was on vacation brought in a young child who was ill.

The resort was filled to capacity, but rather then turning them away, Mr. Boldt willingly gave up his room. They were so impressed by his service and selflessness, the Astors immediately thought of Mr. Boldt as a general manager when they constructed the Waldorf-Astoria.[4]

Mr. Boldt demonstrated the importance of selflessness as a servant leader. His willingness to give up his room to attend to a sick child gave him the opportunity to lead one of the greatest hotels in America, and his selflessness is still being replicated in its employees to date.

You likely have your own examples of selflessness that come to mind. Perhaps a parent, a teacher, a sibling, or a friend inspires you. For us, George Boldt and Pastor O. A. Alderson have set the bar of selflessness!

REFLECTION QUESTIONS

1. Looking at how selflessness is threaded through the traits of a servant leader, can you think of a leader who embodies this trait?

2. Pastor O drew people to him because he poured everything he had back into them. How can you, as a servant leader, mirror this with the people in your life?

3. Mr. Boldt gave up his own comfort to help a customer in need. Are you willing to give up comforts in your life to help those in need?

ACTION SUGGESTION

Give up something important to you today. For some it may be your morning cup of coffee; buy one for someone else instead. For others, it may be buying a fashionable piece of clothing or a bag. Consider spending the money by buying something for someone in need or donating the money to an organization that helps those in crisis.

CHAPTER NINETEEN

SERVICE IS A SACRIFICE

"I think that the good and the great are only separated by the willingness to sacrifice."

—KAREEM ABDUL-JABBAR
(THE NBA'S ALL-TIME LEADING SCORER)

IMAGINE COMING HOME FROM a war in Afghanistan, or Iraq, or—years ago, Vietnam, or Korea—with one leg missing. Or one leg and one arm gone. Or both legs. Or both legs and both arms. Worse yet, imagine coming home in a flag-draped box.

Now imagine that you were the leader who led your troops into battle, and lost your limbs or your life because you threw your own body in front of your followers, in order to save their lives.

This scenario is not difficult to imagine. Something very similar has happened in every war since the dawn of recorded history.

The leaders who give their all in the process of leadership are the ultimate servant leaders. They place their followers—those they serve—above themselves. They understand a timeless but difficult teaching: "No one has greater love than someone who is willing to give his or her life for a friend."

While servant leadership often requires that we set aside some of our comforts and conveniences, there are undeniable rewards that result from our sacrifices. We believe those rewards form the foundation of true living. Every time something we do changes someone else's life, even in the simplest of ways, we know that we have done the right thing. John Maxwell talks about the sacrifices a good leader makes, "Usually, the higher that leader has climbed, the greater the sacrifices he has made. Effective leaders sacrifice much that is good in order to dedicate themselves to what is best. Sacrifice is a constant in leadership."[1]

In his bestselling book, Holocaust survivor and psychologist Viktor Frankel discusses the reality that life begins to have meaning and purpose when one commits to living their life for others. Frankel writes, "Being human always points, and is directed, to something, or someone, other than oneself—be it a meaning to fulfill or another human being to encounter. The more one forgets himself—by giving himself to a cause to serve or another to love— the more human he is and the more he actualizes himself."[2]

Our simple, straightforward objective in writing this book, which we consider a "very personal letter" to you, was to demonstrate that servant leaders impact the world every day in unimaginable ways. Servant leaders touch lives—one at a time, or many all at once. And you can join their ranks!

People often believe that real leaders are extraordinary people who live in extraordinary times and do extraordinary things. But in reality, the real leaders among us are the servant leaders. "Anytime we give of ourselves and our resources, anytime we give from the heart with the intention to help another human being, we sacrifice."[3] This is the heart of being a servant leader.

As we've tried to make very clear, servant leaders are not the rich and powerful, nor the kings and queens, nor the presidents and politicians of the world. Not for the most part, anyway. As we've tried to demonstrate in these pages, the reality is they may even be the poor and the unknown of the world. Often, they are ordinary people living ordinary lives in ordinary circumstances. They are teachers and mechanics. They are farmers and stay-at-home moms. They are bankers and grocers and students and Boys and Girls Clubs volunteers. In other words, they are *you*.

> **"**
> Servant leaders touch lives—one at a time, or many all at once.

Some of you may have read the book or seen the movie, The Hiding Place. This is the true story of Corrie ten Boom, her sister, Betsie, her father, Casper, and other members of her family.

The ten Boom family lived in Haarlem, Holland, where they enjoyed simple lives as watchmakers. Corrie herself was the first woman in Holland to become a certified watchmaker. The family lived on the upper floors of the clock shop they owned.

When the Nazis stormed into the Netherlands during World War II, all Jewish citizens were in immediate jeopardy. Unwilling to accept the horrors that were forced upon their friends and neighbors, the ten Booms built a secret room on the uppermost

> **"Jesus, as an example of servant leadership, still holds up under the closest scrutiny.**

floor of their shop/home. They hid people in this room until their "guests" could be smuggled out of the country to safety. Hundreds of lives were saved through the sacrificial servant leadership of the ten Boom family.

Their plan worked flawlessly until their activities were discovered. Operatives of the Gestapo forced their way into the ten Boom home, and the entire family was sent to a local prison. Corrie and Betsie were then packed into a cattle car on a train, and ended up in Ravensbruuk concentration camp. Betsie died there; Casper and other family members died in other death camps. Only Corrie survived.

After her release, Corrie ten Boom traveled the world telling audiences through speeches—and eventually through her book and the movie—that "No pit is so deep that [God] is not deeper still."

A tree was planted in Corrie's honor at the Holocaust Memorial in Jerusalem in 1968. It grew proud and tall on the Avenue of Righteous Gentiles, in the same garden where a tree also honored Oskar Schindler. We've been told that on the very day Corrie died—April 15, 1993, her ninety-first birthday—her tree died, too.

THE PERFECT EXAMPLE OF SERVANT LEADERSHIP

Corrie exemplified the traits of servant leadership as beautifully and completely—we believe—as any human being is capable of achieving. But for us, there is one supreme example, and that is Jesus of Nazareth, who many of us believe to be the Messiah promised in the Tanakh.

You may not believe that at all, but Jesus, as an example of servant leadership, still holds up under the closest scrutiny. Even if you don't accept that He was the Son of God, you probably agree that He lived 2,000 years ago, that He gathered loyal followers who were willing to die for His cause, and that His profound teachings have impacted the world.

You might also venture that other prophets, spiritual leaders, and religions have had global impact, but we believe Jesus Christ stands apart for many sound reasons—the principal one being His clear example of servant leadership.

Consider how He demonstrated the traits we've discussed:

He had vision: He said, "I came to find and restore the lost,"[4] and "I came to serve not to be served."[5]

He had values: When Satan led him into the barren desert for forty days, He was tempted: "Speak the word that will turn these stones into bread."[6] And, "The kingdoms of the world are yours. Just go down on your knees and worship me, and they're yours."[7] But Jesus had the values and the teachings of the Old Testament to guide Him. "It takes more than bread to stay alive." He said. "It takes a steady stream of words from God's mouth."[8] And, he quoted one of the Ten Commandments: "It is written: 'Worship the Lord your God, and only Him.'"[9]

He displayed faithfulness: He loved his friends deeply, and helped them in miraculous ways. When he approached the grave of his friend, Lazarus, he wept over him. But then he raised Lazarus from the dead. He called out to Lazarus in the tomb, and, sure enough, a living man walked out.[10]

He demonstrated acceptance: He asked a tax collector to follow him—a man named Matthew, who was despised by the citizens from whom he basically extorted money.[11] That changed Matthew's life! He also accepted a man named Zacchaeus, thought of by many as evil, and had dinner at the man's house.[12] He loved people. As a result, He could also accept them.

He was loyal. Not only was Jesus loyal to His disciples—even though they disappointed Him on many occasions—but He was also loyal to His calling as a servant leader. In Luke 2:41–52, you'll find one of the few accounts of His childhood.

> *Every year Jesus' parents traveled to Jerusalem for the Feast of Passover. When he was twelve years old, they went up as they always did for the Feast. When it was over and they left for home, the child Jesus stayed behind in Jerusalem, but his parents didn't know it. Thinking he was somewhere in the company of pilgrims, they journeyed for a whole day and then began looking for him among relatives and neighbors. When they didn't find him, they went back to Jerusalem looking for him.*
>
> *The next day they found him in the Temple seated among the teachers, listening to them and asking questions. The teachers were all quite taken with him, impressed with the sharpness of his answers. But his parents were not impressed; they were upset and hurt.*
>
> *His mother said, "Young man, why have you done this to us? Your father and I have been half out of our minds looking for you."*
>
> *He said, "Why were you looking for me? Didn't you know that I had to be here, dealing with the*

things of my Father?" But they had no idea what he was talking about.

So he went back to Nazareth with them, and lived obediently with them. His mother held these things dearly, deep within herself. And Jesus matured, growing up in both body and spirit, blessed by both God and people.

He was humble. He was the only Son of God (John 3:16), yet He was baptized by His cousin John.

Jesus then appeared, arriving at the Jordan River from Galilee. He wanted John to baptize him. John objected, "I'm the one who needs to be baptized, not you!"

But Jesus insisted. "Do it. God's work, putting things right all these centuries, is coming together right now in this baptism." So John did it.

The moment Jesus came up out of the baptismal waters, the skies opened up and he saw God's Spirit— it looked like a dove—descending and landing on him. And along with the Spirit, a voice: "This is my Son, chosen and marked by my love, delight of my life." (Matthew 3:13–17)

He had integrity. He promoted higher standards. He taught that hating someone was the equivalent of wanting to murder them.[13] And that thinking about seducing someone else's wife or husband was the same as adultery.[14] And that it's easy to love those who love us—but that loving our enemies is a higher standard worth pursuing.[15]

He showed compassion, by willingly going where He was needed, healing the sick, and, yes, even raising the dead. Here is one such account from Matthew 9:18–26:

> *A local official appeared, bowed politely, and said, "My daughter has just now died. If you come and touch her, she will live." Jesus got up and went with him, his disciples following along.*
>
> *Just then a woman who had hemorrhaged for twelve years slipped in from behind and lightly touched his robe. She was thinking to herself, "If I can just put a finger on his robe, I'll get well." Jesus turned—caught her at it. Then he reassured her: "Courage, daughter. You took a risk of faith, and now you're well." The woman was well from then on.*
>
> *By now they had arrived at the house of the town official, and pushed their way through the gossips looking for a story and the neighbors bringing in casseroles. Jesus was abrupt: "Clear out! This girl isn't dead. She's sleeping." They told him he didn't know what he was talking about. But when Jesus had gotten rid of the crowd, he went in, took the girl's hand, and pulled her to her feet—alive. The news was soon out, and traveled throughout the region.*

He offered encouragement. In His "sermon on the mountaintop," He encouraged those who have lost hope, the discouraged, the persecuted, and those who care (Matthew 5:3–10). Later, in Matthew 11:28–30, He gave these promises to those who choose to follow Him:

"Are you tired? Worn out? Burned out on religion? Come to me. Get away with me and you'll recover your life. I'll show you how to take a real rest. Walk with me and work with me—watch how I do it. Learn the unforced rhythms of grace. I won't lay anything heavy or ill-fitting on you. Keep company with me and you'll learn to live freely and lightly."

He taught generosity, by giving the greatest, most generous gift imaginable—Himself. Here is the account of His last Passover meal with His followers:

During the meal, Jesus took and blessed the bread, broke it, and gave it to his disciples:
  "Take, eat.
  This is my body."
  Taking the cup and thanking God, he gave it to them:
  "Drink this, all of you.
  This is my blood,
  God's new covenant poured out for many people
for the forgiveness of sins.
  "I'll not be drinking wine from this cup again until that new day when I'll drink with you in the kingdom of my Father." (Matthew 26:26–29)

Jesus set the ultimate standard of love and generosity when He said:

"This is my command: Love one another the way I loved you. This is the very best way to love. Put your life on

the line for your friends. You are my friends when you do the things I command you. I'm no longer calling you servants because servants don't understand what their master is thinking and planning. No, I've named you friends because I've let you in on everything I've heard from the Father." (John 15:13–15)

Jesus illustrated and encouraged respect. He not only taught respect for people from all walks of life—even, as we mentioned earlier, by refusing to condemn a woman who was caught in the act of adultery—but rather encouraging her to turn away from her old life (John 8:1–11). He also taught respect for the temple—the house of God.

> *Jesus went straight to the Temple and threw out everyone who had set up shop, buying and selling. He kicked over the tables of loan sharks and the stalls of dove merchants. He quoted this text:*
> *"My house was designated a house of prayer;*
> *You have made it a hangout for thieves."*
> *Now there was room for the blind and crippled to get in. They came to Jesus and he healed them. (Matthew 21:12–14)*

Jesus did what He had to do—even those things that were "unpopular," in order to serve everyone, especially those in need of healing.

He mentored His followers. The written record of Jesus' spoken words and His actions is contained in the New Testament. Much of the account relates specifically to those things He taught to His closest followers—His disciples—in one-on-one, one-on-two-or-three, or one-on-twelve sessions.

His twelve key followers—His Disciples—were given the following advice as He was about to send them out to do His work:

> *"Don't begin by traveling to some far-off place to convert unbelievers. And don't try to be dramatic by tackling some public enemy. Go to the lost, confused people right here in the neighborhood. Tell them that the kingdom is here. Bring health to the sick. Raise the dead. Touch the untouchables. . . .*
>
> *"Don't think you have to put on a fund-raising campaign before you start. You don't need a lot of equipment. You are the equipment, and all you need to keep that going is three meals a day. Travel light.*
>
> *"When you enter a town or village, don't insist on staying in a luxury inn. Get a modest place with some modest people, and be content there until you leave.*
>
> *"When you knock on a door, be courteous in your greeting. If they welcome you, be gentle in your conversation. If they don't welcome you, quietly withdraw. Don't make a scene. Shrug your shoulders and be on your way. . . .*
>
> *"Stay alert. This is hazardous work I'm assigning you. You're going to be like sheep running through a wolf pack, so don't call attention to yourselves. Be as cunning as a snake, inoffensive as a dove.*
>
> *"Don't be naive. Some people will impugn your motives, others will smear your reputation—just because you believe in me. Don't be upset when they*

haul you before the civil authorities. Without knowing it, they've done you—and me—a favor, given you a platform for preaching the kingdom news! And don't worry about what you'll say or how you'll say it. The right words will be there; the Spirit of your Father will supply the words.

"When people realize it is the living God you are presenting and not some idol that makes them feel good, they are going to turn on you, even people in your own family. There is a great irony here: proclaiming so much love, experiencing so much hate! But don't quit. Don't cave in. It is all well worth it in the end. It is not success you are after in such times but survival. Be survivors!...

"A student doesn't get a better desk than her teacher. A laborer doesn't make more money than his boss. Be content—pleased, even—when you, my students, my harvest hands, get the same treatment I get. If they call me, the Master, 'Dungface,' what can the workers expect?

"Don't be intimidated. Eventually everything is going to be out in the open, and everyone will know how things really are. So don't hesitate to go public now.

"Don't be bluffed into silence by the threats of bullies. There's nothing they can do to your soul, your core being." (Matthew 10:5–28)

These words are as applicable for servant leaders today as they were 2,000 years ago!

Jesus lived a life of flexibility. He was visiting in someone's home when a paralyzed man's friends cut a hole in the roof and lowered their friend right down in front of Jesus. He stopped what He was doing and immediately healed the disabled man.[16]

He was an amazing example of resilience. Here is the account of his last days; excerpts from Luke 23:32–43:

> *Two others, both criminals, were taken along with him for execution.*
>
> *When they got to the place called Skull Hill, they crucified him, along with the criminals, one on his right, the other on his left.*
>
> *Jesus prayed, "Father, forgive them; they don't know what they're doing."*
>
> *Dividing up his clothes, they threw dice for them. The people stood there staring at Jesus, and the ringleaders made faces, taunting, "He saved others. Let's see him save himself! The Messiah of God—ha! The Chosen—ha!"...*
>
> *One of the criminals hanging alongside cursed him: "Some Messiah you are! Save yourself! Save us!"*
>
> *But the other one made him shut up: "Have you no fear of God? You're getting the same as him. We deserve this, but not him—he did nothing to deserve this."*
>
> *Then he said, "Jesus, remember me when you enter your kingdom."*
>
> *He said, "Don't worry, I will. Today you will join me in paradise."*

A man who was about to die from execution on a rough wooden cross asked His Father to forgive His killers. That is some kind of resilience!

But all of these examples of servant leadership pale in comparison to His demonstration of selflessness.

Jesus agreed with God His Father that something needed to be done to rescue humanity from the painful ravages of a world gone crazy with selfishness. He was willing to say, "I will give up the wonders of heaven to be born among humans, to live the life of a human, to die like a human. I am willing to be the ultimate servant leader, because you—and because I—love those men and women and children so much."

Here's what Paul, a follower of Jesus who formerly persecuted Christians, had to say in Philippians 2:6–8:

> *Think of yourselves the way Christ Jesus thought of himself. He had equal status with God but didn't think so much of himself that he had to cling to the advantages of that status no matter what. Not at all. When the time came, he set aside the privileges of deity and took on the status of a slave, became human! Having become human, he stayed human. It was an incredibly humbling process. He didn't claim special privileges. Instead, he lived a selfless, obedient life and then died a selfless, obedient death—and the worst kind of death at that—a crucifixion.*

And here's what Jesus had to say, beginning with John 3:16:

> *"This is how much God loved the world: He gave his Son, his one and only Son. And this is why: so that no one need be destroyed; by believing in him, anyone can have a whole and lasting life. God didn't go to all the*

trouble of sending his Son merely to point an accusing
finger, telling the world how bad it was. He came to help,
to put the world right again. Anyone who trusts in him
is acquitted; anyone who refuses to trust him has long
since been under the death sentence without knowing it.
And why? Because of that person's failure to believe in
the one-of-a-kind Son of God when introduced to him."

You've undoubtedly been to some event—an NFL football game, perhaps—where someone in the crowd held up a sign in the end zone that read "John 3:16." Chances are, that person is not some kind of nut case who wanted to bring attention to himself or herself.

No, believe it or not, that person is actually a servant leader who believes in the principles we have described in this book. That person has discovered the peace and joy and forgiveness that come from inviting the ultimate Servant Leader into your life.

The thing is, many people on this earth don't have any interest in becoming servants. They don't want to give of themselves. They are more interested in taking.

The reason for this is something called *sin*. Terrible word, isn't it? Really dumb-sounding. It seems so old-fashioned, so out-of-date, so "religious."

What the term *sin* really means is "not fully living up to God's idea of who we are capable of being." It means "we want our own way."

> The thing is, many people on this earth don't have any interest in becoming servants. They don't want to give of themselves.

The reason we know this is that we—Rich and Robyn Wilkerson—are sinners who needed and accepted the forgiveness that Jesus offered us.

If our own current behaviors—and memories of our past behaviors—weren't enough to convince us, the words of the Bible did.

Since we've compiled this long and sorry record as sinners and proved that we are utterly incapable of living the glorious lives God wills for us, God did it for us. Out of sheer generosity he put us in right standing with himself. A pure gift. He got us out of the mess we're in and restored us to where he always wanted us to be. And he did it by means of Jesus Christ. (Romans 3:23–24)

Here's a reality check, though. Following Jesus Christ and accepting His free gift of forgiveness and eternal life will never make you perfect.

We can all point to things that Christians do that disappoint us and even break our hearts. No one on earth will ever be perfect. If they claim that to be true, don't believe them for a minute. Jesus says:

"Be wary of false preachers who smile a lot, dripping with practiced sincerity. Chances are they are out to rip you off some way or other. Don't be impressed with charisma; look for character. Who preachers are is the main thing, not what they say. A genuine leader will never exploit your emotions or your pocketbook." (Matthew 7:15–19)

You will probably never meet a perfect person. Not a perfect parent, not a perfect teacher, and especially not a perfect pastor—or a perfect Christian.

But if you look for them, you will find servant leaders: people who have big hearts even if they have small bank accounts. They are ordinary people following the one Servant Leader who can inspire them and motivate them to be part of the servant leadership solution.

REFLECTION QUESTIONS

1. History is full of people who were willing to sacrifice everything to help others. Jesus is the ultimate example. What are you willing to sacrifice as a servant leader?

2. Jesus is the ultimate example of a servant leader. How can you incorporate His examples into your life?

ACTION SUGGESTION

Read through the Scripture verses in this chapter again and thank Jesus for being the ultimate Servant Leader.

CHAPTER TWENTY

LET TODAY BE YOUR BEGINNING!

"If you really want to do something, you'll find a way.
If you don't, you'll find an excuse."

—JIM ROHN

"I DON'T HAVE TIME. REALLY."

"I'm busy."

"My job demands everything from me."

"I just got married."

"I have responsibility to my family."

"I have to pay college loans (mine or my kids')."

The truth is, there is never a perfect time to be a servant leader. In fact, there is never even a convenient time.

But one day, we all arrive at the point of our last, and most inconvenient, excuse: "I'm dead."

Yet, as we go through life, it generally occurs to all of us that we want to have a lasting legacy. We want to be remembered for doing something great—or at least something meaningful.

Most of us will never give enough money to a university to have a building named after us. Most of us will never be movie stars, recording stars, or bestselling authors. Most of us will never win Wimbledon or wear a World Series or Super Bowl ring.

The best way for most of us to leave a legacy is to leave a lasting impact on the people in our lives, by serving them, even when it's inconvenient. But how do we get involved in servant leadership? What do we really have to offer? What do we need to be willing to actually *do?*

The key to servant leadership is to ASK.

HOW TO GET INVOLVED

By ASK we mean, look for opportunities and pursue them.

Jesus made this clear in Luke 11:9: *"Here's what I'm saying: Ask and you'll get; seek and you'll find; knock and the door will open."*

Do you see this? If you desire to become a servant leader, there are three components to ASK.

Ask: Make your request, make it clear, and expect a response. The first question to ask is, "Do you need help?" The second is, "How can *I* help?"

Seek: It may take you some time to find the ideal—if not perfect—opportunity for you to serve. If you run into roadblocks, don't stop looking. There are too many needs in the world . . . and too few leaders willing to serve.

Knock: No door will open for you if you don't knock (or ring the doorbell) first. Be brave. Knock on doors.

Knock on the door of a service organization—Lions, Kiwanis, Rotary, and the like—and ask if they are looking for members.

Knock on the door of a charity—heart, cancer, Leukemia/Lymphoma, boys' clubs, girls' clubs, a homeless shelter—and announce "I'm here. I'm available. What do you need?"

Knock on the door of a school. "Do you need my skills? Can I support the band? Can I sell tickets at games? Can I tutor students in reading?"

> **"**
> You are a gifted individual. Now it's time to use those gifts in service to others.

Knock on the door of your church, synagogue, mosque, or temple: "What can I do to make a difference?" All faiths need servant leaders.

HOW TO USE THE GIFTS YOU ALREADY HAVE

You are a gifted individual. Now it's time to use those gifts in service to others.

Abilities: These are the gifts you have had nearly from the moment you were born. Can you run fast, jump high? Are you gifted with eye-hand coordination? Can you sing in tune? You can use these gifts somewhere!

Interests: You may have interests that you haven't yet developed or used. As a servant leader, you might even be able to develop those interests in partnership with another person who has similar interests.

Special Skills: Special skills are things you may have developed over time—out of either interest or necessity. We have a friend who had no idea that he had latent carpentry skills, until he finished the basement in his own home. The result was so beautiful that he decided to serve his church by helping build offices in an undeveloped part of their building.

Education: If you have been blessed with an education—any education, not necessarily a formal one—you can pass what you've learned on to others.

Connections: By this, we mean the people you know. Your contacts. There's an old saying: "It's not *what* you know, it's *who* you know." Even if you don't think of yourself as having special abilities, interests, skills, or education, you may have connections that are immeasurably valuable.

Our point is simply this: There are endless ways that you can serve, that you can lead, that you can change lives.

Begin now—and watch what happens!

Everyday people really *can* become extraordinary servant leaders.

Any one of you.

Anywhere you are.

Any time you choose.

Choose today!

Servant leadership is an idea that is right for right now!

REFLECTION QUESTIONS

1. What are the three components to ASK? How would you take these steps?

2. How are you gifted? What abilities, interests, special skills, or connections do you have that you aren't using?

ACTION SUGGESTION

List a skill that you would like to improve or develop in your life. Next, make a list of things you can do this week to make that happen.

ENDNOTES

INTRODUCTION

1. Ruma Bose and Lou Faust, *Mother Teresa, CEO* (San Francisco, CA: Berrett-Koehler Publishers, 2011).

CHAPTER ONE: SQUARE ONE

1. Richard F. Bowman, "Teacher as Servant Leader," *Clearing House* 78, no. 6 (2005): 257–259.

2. "Q & A: Health Care for the Poorest as a Central Human Right." *New York Times,* March 29, 2003: 1–2.

3. Matthew 25:35–36

4. Charles Dickens and Michael Cotsell, *Our Mutual Friend* (Oxford, England: Oxford UP, 2008).

5. John C. Maxwell, *The Right to Lead* (Nashville, TN: Thomas Nelson, 2009).

6. J. T. Whetstone, "Personalism and Moral Leadership: The Servant Leader with a Transforming Vision." *Business Ethics: A European Review* 11, no. 4 (2002): 385–392.

1. Harold Geneen and Alvin Moscow, *Managing* (Garden City, NY: Doubleday, 1984).

2. Martin Luther King, Jr., "The Drum Major Instinct" at Ebenezer Baptist Church February 4, 1968. *The King Center.* http://www.thekingcenter.org/archive/document/drum-major-instinct-ebenezer-baptist-church (accessed June 9, 2013).

3. Agnes Teh, "Boy, 7, raises $240,000 for Haiti appeal." *CNN World.* http://www.cnn.com/2010/WORLD/europe/01/25/uk.boy.charity.haiti/index.html (accessed July 20, 2013).

4. Chris Hodges, *Fresh Air* (Tulsa: Tyndale House Publishers, Inc., 2012).

5. Bose, *Mother Teresa.*

6. J. M. Burns, *Leadership* (New York: Harper & Row, 1978).

7. Eugene H. Peterson, *Run with the Horses* (Madison: Intervarsity Press, 1983).

CHAPTER THREE: THE TRAITS OF THE SERVANT LEADER

1. Michael Agnes and David B. Guralnik, *Webster's New World College Dictionary* (Cleveland: Wiley Publishers, 2007).

2. Virtual thesaurus

3. James A. Autry, *The Servant Leader* (New York: Three Rivers Press, 2001).

4. Larry W. Boone and Sanya Makhani, "Five Necessary Attitudes of a Servant Leader," *Review of Business* 33, no. 2 (Winter 2012): 83–96.

CHAPTER FOUR: VISION

1. Ken Blanchard and Phil Hodges, *The Servant Leader* (Nashville: Thomas Nelson Inc., 2003).

2. Michael Bell and Sylvia Habel, "Coaching for a Vision for Leadership: Oh the Places We'll Go and the Thinks We Can Think," *International Journal of Reality Therapy* 29, no. 1 (Fall 2009): 18–23.

3. James M. Kouzes and Barry Z. Posner. *The Leadership Challenge,* 4th edition (San Francisco: John Wisley and Sons, Inc., 2007).

4. Warren Bennis and Burt Nanus, *Leaders: Strategies for Taking Charge* (New York: HarperCollins Publishers, 2007).

5. Steven Furtick, *Greater* (Colorado Springs, Multnomah Books, 2012).

6. James W. Sipe and Don M. Frick, *Seven Pillars of Servant Leadership* (Paulist Press: Mahwah, New Jersey 2009).

CHAPTER FIVE: VALUES

1. Chuck Salter, "Chick-fil-A's Recipe for Customer Service." *Fast Company.* http://www.fastcompany. com/resources/customer/chickfila.html (accessed June 20, 2013).

2. Mark D. Bennett and Joan McIver Gibson, *A Field Guide to Good Decisions* (Westport, CT: Greenwood Publishing Group, Inc., 2006).

3. Dave Ramsey, "Financial Peace for the EntreLeader, Part 2 with Rabbi Daniel Lapin." *The EntreLeadership Podcast.* http://www.daveramsey. com/entreleadership/podcast.

4. Robert P. Neuschel, *The Servant Leader* (Evanston, IL: Northwestern University Press, 2005).

CHAPTER SIX: FAITHFULNESS

1. Gary J. Bredfeldt, *Great Leader, Great Teacher: Recovering the Biblical Vision for Leadership* (Chicago: Moody Publishers, 2006).

2. Larry Bossidy and Ram Charan, *Execution: The Discipline of Getting Things Done* (New York: Crown Business, 2002).

3. Jon P. Howell, *Snapshots of Great Leadership* (New York: Routledge, 2013).

4. Bennis, *Leaders.*

5. John Evan Smith, *Booth the Beloved: Personal Recollections of William Booth, Founder of the Salvation Army* (London: Oxford University Press, 1949).

6. "Mission Statement & Core Values." *Convoy of Hope.* http://www.convoyofhope.org/go/who/mission_statement_core_values

7. Anderson Cooper, "Convoy of Hope," *Anderson Cooper 360* November 9, 2012. http://www.cnn.com/

8. Tony Blair, *My Journey: My Political Life* (New York: Vintage Books, 2010).

CHAPTER SEVEN: ACCEPTANCE

1. William Shakespeare and Norman Norwood Holland, *Henry IV, with New and Updated Critical Essays and a Revised Bibliography* (New York: Signet Classics, 2002).

2. Tim Lavender, *Achieving Personal Greatness: Discover the 10 Powerful Keys to Unlocking Your Potential* (Nashville: Thomas Nelson, Inc., 2002).

3. Keith Craft, *Leadershipology 101* (San Francisco: Leadership Shapers, 2009).

4. Mark Batterson, *In a Pit with a Lion on a Snowy Day: How to Survive and Thrive When Opportunity Roars* (Colorado Springs: Multonomah Books, 2006).

5. David L. Goetsch, *Developmental Leadership: Equipping, Enabling, and Empowering Employees*

for Peak Performance (Bloomington, IN: Trafford Publishing, 2011).

CHAPTER EIGHT: LOYALTY

1. 1 Samuel 18:1

2. 1 Samuel 18:7–9

3. 1 Samuel 18:12–16

4. Denny Duron, *The Abishai Anointing* (Shreveport: Denny Duron Evangelistic Association, 2003).

5. Bramble, R. L. *Leadership Lessons from the Bible: 40 Timeless Principles for 21st Century Leaders.* San Antonio, TX: Xulon Press, 2005.

6. Autry, *Servant Leader.*

CHAPTER NINE: HUMILITY

1. Patrick Leoncioni, "The Greatest Leader," in *Pat's Point of View: A Collection of Essays on Leadership and Management* (Lafayette, CA: The Table Group, 2011), 70.

2. Gregory K. Morris, *In Pursuit of Leadership* (USA: Xulon Press, 2006).

3. Numbers 12:3

4. Patrick Leoncioni, "Stooping to Greatness," in *Pat's Point of View: A Collection of Essays on Leadership*

and Management (Lafayette, CA: The Table Group, 2011), 8.

5. Antony Bell, *Great Leadership* (Mountain View, CA: Davies-Black Publishing, 2006).

CHAPTER TEN: INTEGRITY

1. Charles P. Garcia, *Leadership Lessons of the White House Fellows* (New York: McGraw Hill, 2009).

2. Wilfredo, De Jesus, *Amazing Faith* (Springfield, MO: Influence Resources, 2012).

3. Ken Blanchard and Phil Hodges, *Lead Like Jesus* (Nashville: Thomas Nelson, Inc., 2005).

4. Barry Gibbons, *This Indecision Is Final* (Chicago: Irwin Professional Publisher, 1996).

5. Craig Groeschel, *Alter Ego* (Grand Rapids: Zondervan, 2013).

6. Dallas Willard, *Renovation of the Heart* (Colorado Springs: Navpress, 2002).

CHAPTER ELEVEN: COMPASSION

1. Luke 10:30–36

2. Dino Rizzo, *Servolution* (Grand Rapids: Zondervan, 2009).

3. Walter Earl Fluker, *Ethical Leadership* (Minneapolis: Augsburg Fortress, 2009).

4. Ibid.

5. Brian Jarrett, *Extravagant* (Springfield, MO: Influence Resources, 2011).

CHAPTER TWELVE: ENCOURAGEMENT

1. Don C. Dinkmeyer and Daniel G. Eckstein, *Leadership by Encouragement* (Boca Raton, FL: CRC Press LLC, 1996.)

2. John C. Maxwell, *The 17 Indisputable Laws of Teamwork* (Nashville: Thomas Nelson, Inc., 2001.)

3. John C. Maxwell, *Encouragement Changes Everything* (Nashville: Thomas Nelson, 2008).

4. Reid Lamport, *Unleashing the Power of Encouragement* (San Antonio, TX: Xulon Press, 2011).

CHAPTER 13: GENEROSITY

1. Breant Kessel, *It's Not About the Money* (New York: HarperCollins, 2008).

2. Francis Chan, *Crazy Love: Overwhelmed by a Relentless God* (Colorado Springs: David C. Cook, 2008).

3. John Wesley, "Rule of Conduct," in *Letters of John Wesley,* ed. George Eayrs, 1915.

1. Carol S. Pearson, *The Transforming Leader: New Approaches to Leadership for the Twenty-First Century* (San Francisco: Berrett-Koehler Publishers, Inc., 2012).

2. Patrick Leoncioni, "Diversity's Missing Ingredient," in *Pat's Point of View: A Collection of Essays on Leadership and Management* (Lafayette, CA: The Table Group, 2011), 70.

3. T. H. White, *The Books of Merlyn* (Austin: University of Texas Press, 1977).

4. http://www.brainyquote.com/quotes/authors/s/stephen_covey.html

5. Mike Ingram, *The Master Plan: Three Keys to Building a Business and Life With Purpose* (Oklahoma City: Dust Jacket Press, 2012).

6. Bose, *Mother Teresa.*

7. Patrick Lencioni, *The Advantage: Why Organizational Health Trumps Everything Else in Business* (San Francisco: Jossey-Bass, 2012).

CHAPTER FIFTEEN: MENTORING

1. John C. Daresh, *Leader Helping Leaders: A Practical Guide to Administrative Mentoring* (Thousand Oaks, CA: Corwin Press, Inc., 2001).

2. Larry Bossidy and Ram Charan, *Execution: The Discipline of Getting Things Done* (New York: Crown Business, 2002).

3. Tim Sanders, "Love Is the Killer App." *Fast Company.* January 31, 2002. http://www.fastcompany.com/44541/love-killer-app (accessed June 20, 2013).

4. David Clutterbuck, *Everyone Needs a Mentor: Fostering Talent in Your Organisation* (London, UK: CIPD House, 2004).

5. Bill George, *7 Lessons for Leading in Crisis* (San Francisco: Jossey-Bass, 2009).

6. Blanchard, *The Servant Leader.*

7. http://www.britannica.com/EBchecked/topic/760136/Gloria-Macapagal-Arroyo

CHAPTER SIXTEEN: FLEXIBILITY

1. Gary Yukl and Richard Lepsinger, *Flexible Leadership: Creating Value by Balancing Multiple Challenges and Choices* (San Francisco: Jossey-Bass, 2004).

2. Steve Echols and Allen England, *Catastrophic Crisis: Ministry Leadership in the Midst of Trial and Tragedy* (Nashville: B&H Publishing Group, 2011).

3. Jim Collins, *From Good to Great: Why Some Companies Make the Leap and Others Don't* (New York: Harper Collins, 2001).

4. Norris M. Haynes, *Group Dynamics: Basics and Pragmatics for Practitioners* (Lanham, MD: University Press of America, Inc., 2012).

CHAPTER SEVENTEEN: RESILIENCE

1. Salvatore R. Maddi and Deborah M. Khoshaba, *Resilience at Work: How to Succeed No Matter What Life Throws at You* (New York: AMACOM, 2005).

2. Jerry L. Patterson, George A. Goens, and Diane E. Reed, *Resilient Leadership for Turbulent Times: A Guide to Thriving in the Face of Adversity* (Lanham, MD: Rowman & Littlefield Education, 2009).

3. Condoleezza Rice, "Graduation Wisdom for Grown-Ups." *Good Housekeeping.* http://www.goodhousekeeping.com/family/celebrity-interviews/condoleezza-rice-quotes

4. Malcolm Muggeridge, *A Twentieth-Century Testimony* (Nashville: Thomas Nelson Inc., 1978).

CHAPTER EIGHTEEN: SELFLESSNESS

1. Tony Baron, *The Art of Servant Leadership: Designing Your Organization for the Sake of Others* (Tucson, AZ: Wheatmark, 2010).

2. Blanchard, *The Servant Leader.*

3. Dan R. Ebner, *Servant Leadership Models for Your Parish* (Mahwah, NJ: Paulist Press, 2010).

4. "George C. Boldt Obituary." *New York Times,* December 6, 1916. http://boldtcastle.wordpress.com/ stories/obit/

CHAPTER NINETEEN: SERVICE IS A SACRIFICE

1. John C. Maxwell, *The 21 Most Powerful Minutes in a Leader's Day* (Nashville: Thomas Nelson, 2007).

2. Viktor E. Frankl, *Man's Search for Meaning* (New York: First Washington Square Press, 1985).

3. John W. Abell, *Sacrifice: The Essence of Life* (Bloomington, IN: WestBow Press, 2013).

4. Luke 19:10

5. Matthew 20:25–26

6. Matthew 4:3

7. Matthew 4:8–9

8. Matthew 4:4

9. Matthew 4:10

10. John 11:43–44

11. Matthew 9:9–13

12. Luke 19:1–10

13. Matthew 5:27–28

14. Matthew 5:21–26

15. Matthew 5:44

16. Mark 2:1–12

ACKNOWLEDGMENTS

FOR US, IT HAS TO START with family. First of all, we would like to thank our dear families, the Buntains and the Wilkersons, for their love and kindness—especially our mothers, Bonnie Wilkerson and Lorraine Buntain, and our sister, Kathie Hardcastle, who assisted us with proofreading this book.

Next our sons, Jonfulton, who now pastors a church in the Northwest with his wonderful wife, Ashley, and baby girl Izzy; Rich Jr. and his wife Dawn-Chere, who are here with us on staff as executive pastors at Trinity Church; Graham, whose story in this book we hope will move you to action (he also serves with us here in Miami); and our youngest son, Taylor, who is working on his graduate degree at Princeton University in Princeton, New Jersey.

To our fantastic staff and family at Trinity Church: It is our joy to do life with you.

Thanks to Richardy Blanchard, Samuel Ludington, and Jesse Norman, members of our team who helped us gather information for this book.

Thanks to Dr. James Davis and his World Leaders Group, who encouraged us to write on the topic of servant leadership.

Thanks to Dr. Ken Blanchard, whose book *Lead Like Jesus* rocked our world, and who wrote the foreword. Thanks, Ken!

And finally, to our contributor and editor, Steve Gottry, author, coauthor, and screenwriter, and one of the finest writers this side of heaven—"UR the bomb, M8!"

ABOUT THE AUTHORS

SINCE 1972, RICH WILKERSON has been helping people who are in crises of every description. His main function has been as a communicator. From 1980 to 1990, he spoke to 1.5 million students in 1,700 public schools throughout the United States and Canada. He has traveled to twenty-seven countries lecturing on hope, love, and faith. In 1998, he and his wife and children moved to Miami, Florida, to work with those in need. He assumed leadership of Trinity church with about 250 mostly Haitian people. Today over 4,000 people each weekend call Trinity their church home. He also founded the Peacemakers Family Center, a social service organization which has won $24 million in government funding since 2000. He and his wife, Robyn, (the coauthor of this book) live in Miami. They are the blessed parents of four sons, two daughters-in-love, and one grand-darling named Izzy.

Robyn Wilkerson began this journey with her husband Rich in 1973. Her achievements and success include being the vice president of a mortgage banking firm in Sacramento California; co-anchor for the national TV show "Introduction to Life" with her father, the late Dr. Fulton Buntain; and cofounding the Peacemakers Family Center in Miami, Florida. Robyn is currently seeking a doctoral degree with the Assemblies of God Theological Seminary in Springfield, Missouri. She is a dynamic public speaker who has lectured around the world.

For more information about this book and other valuable resources visit www.salubrisresources.com.